TREASURE FROM THE
PAINTED HILLS

TREASURE FROM THE
PAINTED HILLS

A History of Calico, California, 1882–1907

Douglas Steeples

Foreword by
David O. Whitten, Series Adviser

Contributions in Economics and Economic History, Number 205

Greenwood Press
Westport, Connecticut • London

Library of Congress Cataloging-in-Publication Data

Steeples, Douglas W.
  Treasure from the painted hills : a history of Calico, California,
1882–1907 / Douglas Steeples ; foreword by David O. Whitten.
    p. cm.—(Contributions in economics and economic history,
ISSN 0084–9235 ; no. 205)
  Includes bibliographical references and index.
  ISBN 0–313–30836–5 (alk. paper)
  1. Calico (Calif.)—History. I. Title. II. Series.
F869.C146S84 1999
979.4'95—dc21   98–22905

British Library Cataloguing in Publication Data is available.

Library of Congress Catalog Card Number: 98–22905
ISBN: 0–313–30836–5
ISSN: 0084–9235

First published in 1999

Greenwood Press, 88 Post Road West, Westport, CT 06881
An imprint of Greenwood Publishing Group, Inc.

Printed in the United States of America

The paper used in this book complies with the
Permanent Paper Standard issued by the National
Information Standards Organization (Z39.48–1984).

10 9 8 7 6 5 4 3 2 1

With appreciation to my parents,

Marion Wayne Steeples and Dorothy King Steeples

CONTENTS

LIST OF ILLUSTRATIONS

LIST OF MAPS AND TABLES

Maps

Tables

FOREWORD

Interstate 40 begins without fanfare in Knoxville, Tennessee, at the terminus of Interstate 81, crosses the southern United States, and ends abruptly at Barstow, California. Barstow, an unlikely destination for most travelers, hosts a second great highway, Interstate 15, which originates in San Diego and extends through Las Vegas, Nevada; Salt Lake City, Utah; and Butte, Montana; to Waterton-Glacier International Peace Park at the Montana-Canadian border. Eight miles northeast of Barstow, I-15 passes the ghost town of Calico, denoted by a red block on California state highway maps. A tourist attraction now, Calico is likely to host more domestic visitors on a pretty day than ever there were citizens in the once-thriving town.

Unlike deserted villages and hamlets in Europe that memorialize the victims of Nazi brutality, ghost towns in the western United States recall an age when free-wheeling spirits surrendered the comforts of civilization in search of sudden wealth. Houses, stores, and mills tossed up near gold or silver claims declined in tandem with miners' hopes for lucky strikes, disappearing as they had come on wagons and pack animals headed for another mining field. Many towns not carried away burned; Calico burned and was rebuilt three times. A few of these boom settlements bequeathed ghosts, abandoned structures standing as silent reminders of another time. Calico is one such spectre.

The cultivated ghost town is a congruous memorial to Calico's other two lives. Had the silver miners come and gone Calico would be little more than a historical marker beside I-15 North, but a second, less glamorous, discovery rejuvenated the town. Borax, a mundane companion to gold and silver, is nonetheless a valuable industrial mineral, one that revived investment and employment in Calico, that kept the town alive after silver had left it for dead. The white, water-soluble powder or crystals— $Na_2 B_6O_{11}.10H_2O$ (hydrated sodium borate)—are used in tanning and glassmaking. Like the silver that gave birth to Calico, borax was mined, processed, and transported with a minimum of technology and a maximum of human effort. In contrast, a silver mine or borax pit developed in the 1990s is exploited with great expenditures of capital for machinery but relatively small outlays for labor. So few operating technicians are needed that a scattering of house trailers suffices to provide temporary shelter for men and women who easily and quickly drive or fly to centers of civilization during hiatus from work. A century ago when Calico was a mining town, there were no paved roads, no earthmoving machinery, no heavy trucks powered by internal combustion engines. Instead, horses and mules hauled ore-laden wagons to rail sidings: Americans still associate borax with twenty-mule teams drawing heavy wagons through the desert, an association attributable to pioneering image-makers.

Treasure from the Painted Hills: A History of Calico, California, 1882-1907, is Douglas Steeples' requiem for a ghost town. Steeples, who loves the American Southwest, infuses his narrative with enthusiasm for the raw beauty of the land and the tenacity of its inhabitants. Dissatisfied with the Calico marketed to tourists, Steeples has wrapped into one tight discourse the geographic, economic, social, political, and business history of a once-thriving community struggling to survive in primitive conditions and simultaneously forge its rendering of the peculiarly American civilization.

The account opens with a rich description of the landscape that is Calico. "At irregular intervals rugged mountain ranges jut up from the desert floor, serrating the horizon with ridges averaging 4,000 to 7,500 feet high." The mountains tower above valleys, washes, and dry lake beds. "Joshua trees and junipers struggle on higher slopes . . . tamarisks, mesquite, smoke trees trace the edges of dry stream beds." Cold Canadian air reduces temperatures below freezing in winter and the summer sun "can boil to 115, even 120 degrees and more." Blinding sand storms quickly scar paint and distort glass. A forbidding climate notwithstanding, the region bears signs of human passage. On the first of the chapter's two sketch maps that enhance the charm of his description of the region displayed, Steeples shows the lay of the land, the roads, railroads, towns, and landmarks; the second depicts the rock and fault zones responsible for the mineral riches that built Calico.

Chapters 2 and 3 relate the discovery, exploitation, and exhaustion of Calico's silver and borax deposits. A prospector who was himself named

Silver staked the first claim in the Calico region early in 1881. The discovery of silver was part of a broader search for precious metals across the Southwest and in southeastern California particularly. Lowery Silver's Sara, Silver Mill Site, Conglomerated, and Pico mines attracted prospectors and their attendants to Calico as new claims turned the region into a hive of activity. Steeples' claim map illustrates the extent of mining and construction (buildings, mills, roads, and tunnels). Along with mine productivity figures and the costs of removal, hauling, and processing, Steeples estimates the silver production as "about $14 million to $15 million" through the 1890s, and "more than 10 percent of the nation's silver yield, in 1883."

Steeples accords Calico entrepreneurs attention commensurate with their enterprise, depicting them as varied and engaging as the landscape. Former Milwaukeean Henry Harrison Markham marshaled capital from his native city, John Daggett hailed from New York, and "the Silver King Mining Company, Limited [was] incorporated by seven investors in London, England." Developers were not always mine owners but included town planners and the contractors who built the Calico mills, tramways, and trestles—eight photographs reinforce the Chapter 2 narrative.

Calico's silver fortunes were tied as much to the national economy and monetary policy as to nature's endowment. Steeples surveys Americans' experience in the late nineteenth century with monetary gold and silver. After carefully analyzing the costs of mining and processing of Calico silver, he concludes that it was "unprofitable to mine at Calico when silver prices fell below $1.00 [an ounce]." The collapse of the national economy in 1893 and the fall of silver prices to $0.63 an ounce in 1894 dropped the curtain on Calico silver, the first act in a three-act drama.

In 1883 Hugh Barrett Stevens discovered borax in the hills beyond Calico. Stevens' assay chemist, Thomas Price of San Francisco, revealed the borax discovery to William Tell Coleman before alerting his client. Coleman, already holding borax claims in Death Valley, 165 miles from the railroads in Daggett and at Mojave Station, immediately moved to secure title to deposits in Calico, a mere half dozen miles from Daggett. Coleman initiated borax production in Calico but left the industry in 1888 and died five years later. Francis Marion "Borax" Smith assumed the lead in developing several borax sources, including those at Calico. In 1890 the works at Borate—the camp near Calico—produced about 700 tons a month; a year later the output was up to 2,100 tons; during the peak years 1905-1906 it reached 3,900 tons a month.

Until a rail line connected Daggett and Borate in 1898, Smith employed twenty-mule teams every year but one to haul ore to the railroad at Daggett: that year, 1896, he invested $4,500 in a steam tractor to haul the ore. The 2,500 pounds of coal required to fuel a single round trip from mines to rails was probably reason enough to retire "Old Dinah" after one year. A century after her tour of duty in the desert, "Old Dinah" is a curiosity at the Furnace Creek Inn, in Death Valley. When the Borate & Daggett Rail Road was complete, the "Francis" and the "Marion," Heisler locomotives specially geared for managing the steep grade, replaced the mule teams.

A sketch map delineates the borax mines and rail lines that dominated Calico in the years 1898 to 1907. Photographs capture a twenty-mule team on the trail and "Old Dinah" at work, complete with three crewmen and two decorative women. Other photographs show the locomotive Francis; the high trestle on the line to Daggett; the borax reduction works at Marion; a mine crew at Borate; two views of Borate, one including a distant view of Smith's residence; and a portrait photograph of Smith.

"After yielding some 330,000 tons of ore and refined borax worth $20 million, Calico's mines closed in 1907. Smith's workers took up the rails, disassembled buildings, and moved everything to the new location [the Death Valley properties were by that time accessible by railroad], or, in the case of Smith's house, to Ludlow." Completing his chronology of the Calico borax properties at mid-chapter, Steeples turns to the origins of the industries and Smith's multinational organization for producing and distributing borax. "Smith ranked with such other figures as John D. Rockefeller, Andrew Carnegie, and J. P. Morgan, and his Borate operations [were comparable] with pivotal stages in their advance to preeminence." The parallels are not strained. Rockefeller's Standard Oil profited from Lima crude after considerable research revealed a refining method for the Ohio oil that was unlike the standard Pennsylvania crude. Smith managed similar problems with *Colemanite*, the Calico borax. Once developed, practical processing techniques demanded extensive financing, which forced huge production runs to spread costs thin enough to meet competitive prices. When the world market proved inadequate to take off the vast output of borax, Smith and company turned to creative marketing to expand household sales. Advertising and image-making created the still popular vision of Twenty Mule Team Borax.

Treasure from the Painted Hills is more than the story of silver and borax in Calico and the nation at large. Steeples probes beyond mines and mills in search of the soul of community. Wind unseen reveals its passing in twisted trees, hillocked sands, clouded window panes; soul, too, is reflected, but in paintings, letters, newspapers. Chapter 4 addresses images of living community: "Calico Finds Its Voice: The *Calico Print*." The story of the *Print*, a weekly newspaper established by John G. "Johnny" Overshiner in 1882, is as appealing as accounts of silver and borax. Overshiner etched Calico into the history of the Southwest by observing events, by using the news he reported to shape and promote civic awareness and pride. Politically the *Print* adopted "egalitarianism, hostility toward monopolies and excessive concentration of economic power, and suspicion of politicians and government." Nonpartisan politics, however, were cast aside in matters of silver, as the editor accepted the apparent truth that what was good for Calico must be good for the United States.

The *Print* died in the fire of 1887, but not before Overshiner had published an issue of heroic dimension. The newsprint consumed by flames, the last issue of the *Calico Print* was pressed onto bedsheets in what must be a peculiar twist of irony even for a newspaper. Overshiner took his printing press elsewhere, but it found its way to posterity as part of the collection of Calico relics maintained in Buena Park at Knott's Berry Farm.

The reality of Calico's archeology and geography (Chapter 1) sets the stage for the chronicle of a town founded on silver mining (Chapter 2). Steeples introduces the second act of play Calico, featuring borax mining, the entrepreneurship of "Borax" Smith, and the creation of the twenty-mule team image of borax, the desirable consumer good (Chapter 3). The prime image-maker, the *Calico Print*, takes stage center (Chapter 4) as preamble to Steeples' exploration of life in the real Calico, "Saturday Night in Calico: Life in a Mining Camp" (Chapter 5) in contrast to an image of life, act three in the Calico drama, "Remembering Calico: Historical Mirages" (Chapter 6).

Fact and fantasy mingle in the mural, *Saturday Night in Calico, 1881*, a manufactured memory of a community. How far is the mural from reality? There is, of course, no definitive answer, for it was painted more than a half century after Calico's prime and is displayed in the Calico Saloon in Ghost Town, California, 150 miles from Calico. The mural is a touchstone for comparing Calico the 1880s boom town and Calico the ghost town.

Steeples' evocation of life in the working community of Calico and its environs is exhaustive. He describes the people—who they were; where they came from; how they made a living, worshiped, entertained themselves—how they lived and how they died. An examination of public education is complete with a table of expenditures, capital, days of school, and number of students for each year that the Calico school was in operation. Sanitation facilities, waterworks, fire fighting, police protection, and the courts are investigated along with business operations and transportation companies. Beyond recounting the work Calico inhabitants performed, Steeples itemizes incomes and expenditures. A table of commodity prices enhances the narrative, as do photographs of the town, its people, the mail dog, the sheriff. Violent episodes lend credence to the image of Calico as a wild town but not a town out of control:

> The quiet and matter of fact resoluteness of Calico's people in going about their lives represented a kind of unobtrusive heroism. If the story of their shared life is memorable, it is most so in these terms. Calico's settlers were agents of civilization, jagged edges and all. That they succeeded so well comments favorably on their determination even in their unlikely location.

Steeples contrasts the working Calico with the illusory Calico, reviews the store of Wild West images manufactured and distributed by cinema and television, and shows how these created the stereotypical mining town presented at attractions like Calico ghost town. This new Calico, rebuilt to reflect the original, rests on its silver-mining roots. The borax days are lost to Death Valley, where Calico's twenty-mule teams highlight the latter-day carnival that once was the heart of borax mining and processing. Obscured in the image making, to Steeples' chagrin, is the real Calico.

Steeples tells the tale of three Calicos: the silver-mining town, the borax-mining center, and the ghost town. He has researched and carefully written the complete history of a town from its natural setting to its imaginary legacy. His respect for the people who built Calico, who lived and worked there, makes him uncomfortable with a re-creation that could serve a higher function by displaying more reality and less imagination.

Treasure from the Painted Hills is a solid addition to the history of the Southwest and the town of Calico. It is a masterful business and economic history of regional silver mining and of national borax mining, processing, and marketing. Moreover, Steeples has framed his detailed portrayal of Calico in image analysis that raises the narrative above simple description. Steeples' history is treasure from the painted hills.

David O. Whitten, Series Adviser
Contributions in Economics and Economic History

ACKNOWLEDGMENTS

I first visited Calico, in California's Mojave Desert, decades ago. That encounter sparked an interest that grew as time passed. Conversations with some of the old-timers who had direct experience with the area during its years as an active center of silver and borax mining, 1881-1907, inspired, in turn, sustained inquiry and study. Research uncovered a story of unusual richness and interest. The result is this book. I have written for a varied audience. Students, afficionados of Western Americana, and general readers will find here an arresting, readily accessible account. Specialists will meet with material that extends our knowledge not only of Calico, but also of late nineteenth-century Western mining camps. There is information to underpin a work easily twice as long as this one, but I have elected brevity. My intention is to lay bare the essential and most interesting elements of the story and its significance, rather than to succumb to antiquarianism or to offer a mass of extraneous anecdote or detail. Readers who desire to learn more will find in the chapter endnotes and the bibliography ample direction toward the sources to which they may turn.

I owe debts of gratitude to many persons, not all of whom can be listed in a brief statement. Some have passed on; others are still alive. Professors Davis Applewhite and Fletcher Green, respectively of the University of Redlands and the University of North Carolina at Chapel Hill, provided direction in the early stages of my work. Lucy Bell Lane, Leila Riggs, Walter Alf, Lucille Coke, Betty Hornaday, Alberta Osborne, Emery C. and Clara B. McKinney, Ella Pitcher, and Virgie Timmons, all desert pioneers, shared generously of their knowledge. Harrison "Harry" Preston Gower, who held many positions, including that of archivist at the Pacific Coast

Borax Company, provided material available nowhere else. Harold Weber, Jr., of the California Division of Mines and Geology, and J. T. Weakley, for a time owner of the Silver King and the Waterloo mines at Calico, offered aid toward establishing reliable estimates of silver production in the district.

Librarians beyond counting assisted in locating and retrieving obscure sources. My special thanks to John Barr Tompkins of the Bancroft Library, University of California, Berkeley; Rayonia Babel of the library at Aurora University; and Virginia Cairns and Jane Summey of the Mercer University Library for their help. Jim Hofer, Archivist of the County of San Bernardino, directed me to vital sources in his custody. Dorothy "Duffy" Knaus and Bernard McTigue, Special Collections Librarians at the University of Oregon Library, assisted with work in the Ruth Woodman papers, which contain crucial items concerning borax mining in the Calico Mountains.

L. Burr Belden, a tireless writer of carefully crafted historical articles about the Mojave Desert, steered me away from numerous errors, as did Remi Nadeau. Alan Baltazar, until recently the official historian for the Calico County Park, author of *Calico* and editor of Lucy Lane's *Calico Memories*, left a prodigious legacy of research and was generous with his time and knowledge. Bill Tomlinson, curator of the Mojave River Valley Museum, provided indispensable aid in locating photographs. The museum itself was generous in furnishing photographs for use in this book.

I must also note debts to the editors and anonymous referees for several publications, whose comments strengthened various parts of this volume. I am grateful to the editor of the *Historical Society of Southern California Quarterly*, which published a very different version of Chapter 4, and an article on the By-laws of the Calico Mining District. Readers for and the editor of *Essays in Economic and Business History* made important improvements in an article that appeared in that journal in 1995 and highly compressed elements that appear here in Chapters 2 and 3. A different version of Chapter 3, published in *Montana: The Magazine of Western History*, benefitted greatly from comments of the editor and the referees. Will Wright of the University of Southern Colorado and Steve Kaplan of Buffalo State College (New York), who accepted a substantially different version of Chapter 6 for the 1997 program of the Society for the Interdisciplinary Study of Social Imagery, created thereby a forum that generated helpful observations. I owe much to the friendship of Auburn University Professor of Economics David Whitten, an acute student of all facets of business history. Distinguished professor Gloria Ricci Lothrop of California State University, Northridge, offered important encouragement.

So did my colleague at Mercer, professor Tom Scott of the History Department. Our administrative secretary, Debbie Manly, provided outstanding assistance with graphics formatting. Greenwood Publishing Group's fine editors, Cynthia Harris, Ilke Winer, and David Palmer, steered me away from many infelicities of expression and through the shoals that menace authors preparing camera-ready copy.

I am particularly grateful to Mercer University, first for financial support toward completing archival research. Second, for being the kind of institution that values scholarly work of administrative faculty members no less than that of members of the teaching faculty. Provision of released time from decanal responsibilities helped me carry this project to completion. Most of all, for being a university whose president and chief academic officer set scholarly examples for others to follow. It is refreshing to serve at an institution whose president, when asked why he wrote a controversial book, could reply simply, "Well, a university is a place where people write books."

Finally, my profoundest gratitude goes to my best friend, my closest intellectual companion, my wife, Christine Steeples, who alone knows how fully she contributed to the writing of this volume.

Douglas Steeples
Mercer University

Chapter 1

This Remote Solitude

My sensations upon viewing the Great Desert for the first time were certainly peculiar.
George Brewerton, 1853

Extending east from the junction of the Sierra Nevada and the Sierra San Gabriel to the Colorado River, and north from the latter and the Sierra San Bernardino to the Panamint Mountains and Death Valley, the Mojave Desert is one of the most forbidding places in the continental United States. Its floor averages between one thousand and three thousand feet in elevation. Its fifteen thousand square miles contain eleven thousand-foot Telescope Peak, in the Panamint Range, and Bad Water, the lowest point in the western hemisphere at 280 feet below sea level, just a few miles away. A scattering of towns, a few paved roads, two interstate highways, two major railroads, widely-separated ranches, and a number of active and abandoned mines testify to the few changes that people have wrought in this stark region. Even now, place names on maps warn of the dangers of the desert: Sidewinder Mountain and Sidewinder Valley, Deadman Dry Lake, Devil's Playground, Rattlesnake Canyon, Soda Mountains, Dead Mountains, Lava Bed Mountains, Snake Springs.

The Mojave is a big country, a land of expansive views. At irregular intervals rugged mountain ranges jut up from the desert floor, serrating the horizon with ridges averaging 4,000 to 7,500 feet high. Sometimes the result of volcanic action, sometimes of violent faulting, the ranges testify to the tremendous geological forces at work beneath the surface. Between the ranges lie a series of broad, sweeping valleys. Pierced by sinuous canyons that end with huge alluvial fans where floods resulting from occasional summer cloudbursts spread out over the desert surface and drop their heavy burdens of sediment, they appear to be burying themselves in water-borne debris. Through the centers of many of the intervening valleys run washes, which are dry save after infrequent downpours. Playas, the bare beds of former and long-dry lakes, shimmer blindingly in the desert sun. In some instances, the evaporation of Pleistocene lakes has left briny waters saturated with minerals beneath deceptive crystalline playa surfaces.

To many, the scene is desolate. It appears to be a remote solitude. A mid nineteenth-century traveler expressed a common reaction when he recalled how, when he was about to embark on a desert crossing, his "sensations upon viewing the Great Desert for the first time were certainly peculiar. . . ." To others, the aspect is beautiful, but the beauty is austere, at times even menacing.

Vegetation is sparse. Weirdly shaped Joshua trees and junipers struggle on higher slopes. Descending, one encounters expanses of sage, scattered thin patches of grasses, and isolated desert holly plants, which compete with cacti for survival. Tamarisks, mesquite and smoke trees trace the edges of dry stream beds. Closer to sea level, the ugly but well-adapted creosote bush is common. Only at the margins of springs, seeps, or running sweet water is plant life, including even some wild grapes, abundant. Besides the Colorado River, the region contains only two significant streams, both intermittent. The Amargosa River drains into Death Valley. The channel of the Mojave River runs from the north slope of the San Bernardinos some fifty miles to Barstow, then another seventy miles northeastward to the Mojave River Sink near Soda (Dry) Lake. Apart from the banks of the Colorado River, the only considerable stands of native trees growing at lower elevations, cottonwoods and willows, are found along the Mojave. The stream courses at the surface only where bedrock is at a very shallow depth, last at Afton Canyon.   It flows as far as Barstow only during flooding in an unusually wet winter or spring. Into the mid nineteenth century, Indians inhabited the upper reaches of the stream, and small groups could be found near isolated water holes all the way to the villages of the Mojaves on the Colorado River.

Mountains to the west insulate the desert from moisture-bearing winter storms from the Pacific Ocean. Spring and fall can bring indescribably lovely days. Piercing cold fronts sweeping down from Canada can plunge temperatures well below freezing, except at the lowest elevations, in winter. They can even bring rare snowfalls. Most of what precipitation there is normally falls in summer. Then, when temperatures can boil to 115, even 120 degrees or more, rising hot air can produce thermal low pressure centers that pull humid Pacific air to the desert.   As heat draws this moist air upward, towering thunderheads form and march across the glaring sky,

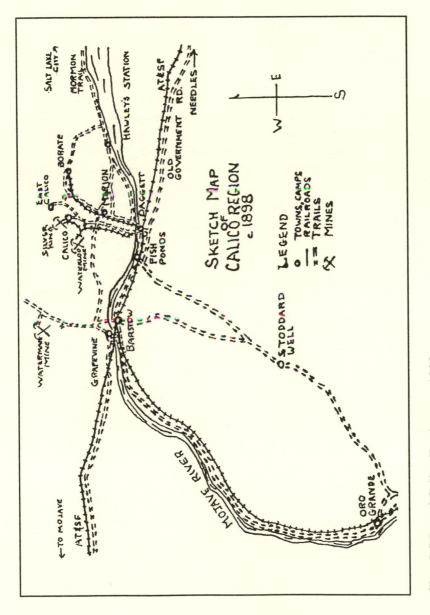

Sketch Map of Calico Region, ca. 1898

drenching local areas in a crazy quilt pattern that can drop one to six inches—a year's total—at one spot while leaving another, a mile away, entirely dry. Sand storms can blow so fiercely that visibility falls to zero, paint is quickly blasted from surfaces, and windows in a very short time become so pitted that they resemble frosted glass.

Long before historic times, Indian trails crossed the desert bearing trade that took highly prized coastal seashells as far inland as central Arizona. In the spring of 1776, friendly Mojaves guided the expedition of Fray Francisco Garces from the Colorado River to the Mission San Gabriel. This trek opened the route to use by Europeans, although Garces crossed the Sierra San Bernardino to the east of what would become the standard path, the Cajon Pass. A half century later, in 1826, Jedediah Smith led the first party of fur traders from the young United States over the same route, repeating his trip a year later. Lt. John Charles Fremont with his second expedition surveyed the trail in 1844. During the Mexican War, Kit Carson carried dispatches over it. By the 1870s, the Old Government Road very largely traced it. In addition, the Mormon Trail branched off and followed a portion of the now largely forgotten Old Spanish Trail, to connect San Bernardino with Salt Lake City via Las Vegas.

In the 1860s and 1870s, a trickle of settlers began to take up land along the Mojave River. Many of these engaged in small-scale farming, drawing water for irrigation from wells. Some of these farms functioned as "stations," where desert travelers could find feed, provisions, rest, and fresh livestock. Among area settlements of the 1870s were Rogers Station (now Victorville), Oro Grande (the site of a gold ore stamping mill), Stoddard Well, Grapevine Station (a bit more than a mile west of modern Barstow), Fish Ponds (on the south side of the Mojave River bed across from the site of the present Barstow Marine Supply Depot), now-vanished Hawley's Station, downstream, and Camp Cady, a few miles to the east, an army post built to guard desert traffic.[1]

The Calico Mountains stand about ten miles to the northeast of Barstow. They rise 2,500 feet above the surrounding desert to the summit of Calico Peak, at just over 4,500 feet. About fifty million years old, they date from the Tertiary (first) period of the Cenozoic, or Recent, age. They originated when chocolate-colored, volcanic mud flows began to disfigure the ancient seabed that forms most of the local desert floor. Subsequent flows, and a series of volcanic uplifts, formed the range itself. Some of the later flows—tuffs, breccias, intrusive andesite, rhyolite, and breccias mixed with conglomerates—attained thicknesses of as much as six hundred to eight hundred feet. Powerful contortions produced numerous fault systems, while

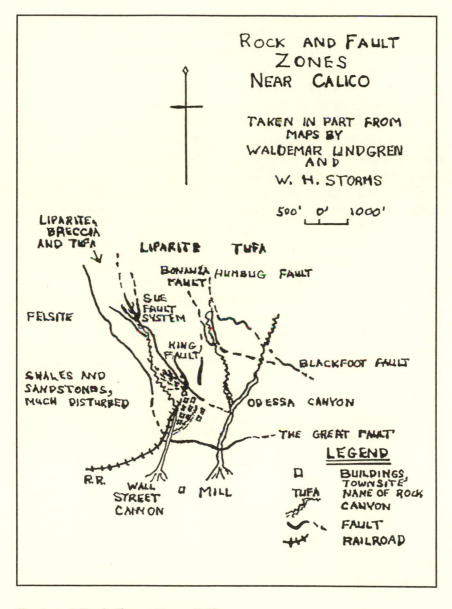

Rock and Fault Zones Near Calico

severely twisting and folding various beds of stratified stone. Almost barren of vegetation, the Calicos abut Calico Dry Lake, which lies immediately to the south. Their axis trends in a northwest-southeast direction for about eight miles. They are half as wide. They received their name because vari-hued mudflows color much of their surface, with reds, lavenders, oranges, yellows, whites, grays, chocolates, tans, greens, and blues.[2]

Wall Street Canyon splits the Calico Mountains, running north along a major fault from the edge of the dry lake. A broad alluvial fan extends from the canyon mouth to the playa. Sage and spidery ocotillo dot the fan. During hot summer days, dust devils vex the surface of the lake. The towering hulk of King Mountain bounds Wall Street Canyon on the east. Beyond lie Odessa and Occidental Canyons. Both are twisting, narrow and sometimes overhung by steep cliffs. Farther on is Mule Canyon, debauches at the east end of the playa and, last, Sunrise Canyon, which opens to the southeast from the far end of the mountains. Save for infrequent forays by prospectors, the Calicos' only human occupants before the 1880s were Indians who lived in temporary camps around Sweetwater Spring above Odessa and Occidental Canyons. This all changed dramatically after 1880 when for a quarter of a century the Calico Mountains became the scene of hectic mining for silver and then for a much less glamorous, but in the end more valuable, industrial mineral, borax. After the mining epoch ended followed another, which persists to the present. This was the epoch of heroic legend-making.

NOTES

1. For early travel across the desert, Leroy R. and Ann W. Hafen, *Old Spanish Trail: Santa Fe to Los Angeles* (Lincoln: University of Nebraska Press, 1993), quoted, 320; for Camp Cady, Leonard B. Waitman, "The History of Camp Cady" (unpublished master's thesis, University of Redlands, 1953); and for stations and the Old Government Road, David G. Thompson, *Routes to Desert Watering Places in the Mohave Desert Region, California* (Washington: Government Printing Office, 1921), and Thompson, *The Old Government Road Across the Mohave Desert to Needles* (San Bernardino: State Emergency Relief Administration, 1939 [author may be listed in some libraries "California, Works Progress Administration"]).

2. For local geology, F. B. Weeks, "Possibilities of the Calico Mining District" (undated manuscript of article of the same title published by the *Engineering and Mining Journal Press*, May 6, 1925); Mary R. Hill, "Silver," *Mineral Information Service*, 16 (Sacramento, June, 1963), 1-8; Harold F. Weber, Jr., "Economic Geology of the Calico District, California," paper presented to Society of Mining Engineers, Las Vegas, Nevada, September 6-8, 1967; Weber, "Silver Deposits of the Calico District," *Mineral Information Service*, 20 (Sacramento, January, 1967), 3-7.

Chapter 2

HORN SILVER

Look here. Pure horn silver.
                                    Charles Mecham, June 27,1881

Lowery Silver staked the first silver claims in the Calico Mountains between January 2 and March 5,1881. His properties, the Conglomerated, Sara, Silver Mill Site, and Pico mines, lay on the northwest edge of the range, about four miles from the site on which the town of Calico shortly grew.[1] In the largest sense his locations were only the most recent chapter in the story of a quest for treasure that dated to Christopher Columbus's voyages to the New World. More proximately, they were part of a process of exploration and mining development that began in the United States with the exploitation of gold finds in North Carolina after 1804. Much larger discoveries in the nearby, heavily wooded mountains of north Georgia in 1829 drew as many as six thousand avid gold seekers through the next half dozen years. With the California rush of 1848 and 1849, the mining fever reached epidemic proportions. It did not subside for half a century. While he was only a bit player in this great drama, Lowery Silver performed his role in circumstances much changed, by the 1880s, from those of his forerunners.

The Georgia mines were important in three ways. Although their output was small, they did furnish the young United States with much needed gold for monetary use. They provided Americans with their first noteworthy experience working with gold ores, creating a pool of knowledgeable miners. And they freshened a lust for mineral wealth that could impel these miners to travel readily to regions from which reports of new discoveries might come. It was no accident that Georgians thronged west and contributed to the development of the California mines.

The gold rush populated California with tens of thousands of immigrants from the eastern United States and many parts of the world and catapulted it to statehood—by-passing territorial status—in 1850. Gold made San Francisco its metropolis, and with discoveries in 1859 of silver in western Nevada and gold in Colorado, loosed a flood of prospectors and miners that for fifty years washed across the West in a restless quest for precious metals.[2] Mining on the public lands, and in California preceding the creation of functioning government, miners founded customs by which to secure and enforce their rights to claims and to the water needed to work the rich Sierra Nevada foothill placer deposits. Through spontaneously formed mining districts, they grounded property rights on the principle of prior appropriation, first in point of time, first in right. They regulated the size of and the manner of marking and of registering claims. They prescribed what improvement work must be performed yearly in order to retain claims. Migrating miners exported California practices to the entire West. These won definitive legal recognition when Congress incorporated them into the federal Mining Law of 1872.[3]

The years following 1848 contained much else that bore on events in the Calico Mountains. Statehood for California heralded the arrival of effective state, county, and local government and law enforcement. San Bernardino, a bustling center of commerce harboring several thousand souls and the seat of the county of the same name, was only eighty-five miles distant. The Mormon Trail and the Old Government Road ran along the Mojave River to a point six miles to the south. There, they forked and continued on to their respective destinations. Each bore a growing burden of traffic, served by several trailside stations. The nearest was at Fish Ponds, on the river eight miles southwest. Los Angeles was within four days by a combination of wagon to Colton or Mojave Station and then railroad, or a week by wagon alone. By 1881, the Atlantic and Pacific, a part of the Santa Fé system, had joined San Diego with San Bernardino and had surveyed a route over the Cajon Pass to the Mojave River. Crews were also building westward across Arizona in a race with the Southern Pacific for control of the Colorado River crossing at The Needles. As of mid-1882, the latter had built thirty-eight miles east of Mojave Station and was advancing "at the rate of three-quarters of a mile a day." By July 1, 1883, it had reached The Needles and had established a station, named Daggett, six miles south of the site on which Calico developed. Despite damage from floods, the Santa Fé system linked San Bernardino to Barstow on November 9,1885, giving Calico one-day rail access to Los Angeles via both Mojave Station and San Bernardino.[4]

Finally, mining itself had matured greatly since 1848. Nowhere was this more evident than in Virginia City, Nevada. Virginia City languished for some years following the initial local discoveries, in 1859. When it boomed in the 1870s, with the opening of fabulous bonanzas, it brought large-scale, capital-intensive, industrial technology and corporate control to western mineral extraction. New methods of timbering; construction of miles of flumes through which water bore millions of board feet of timbers down from the Sierra; the application of steam power to drainage and ventilation, hoisting, and milling; improved milling techniques making use of newly devised mechanical processes; refined smelting methods; and steam railroads joined with capital markets in San Francisco and world markets for gold and silver to sustain the prodigally rich Nevada center.[5] Concurrently, mineral exploration penetrated the entire interior West. Virginia City mines were active between 1859 and 1881, attaining their peak output in the mid-1870s. Silver mining waxed at Cerro Gordo, high in California's barren Inyo range, 1868-1875; at Panamint City, 1873-1876; at Darwin, 1874-1878; at wind-swept Bodie, 1877-1881; at Providence from the 1870s into the 1880s. A half dozen gold mines began operation along the Mojave River thirty-seven miles upstream from the Calico Mountains, at Oro Grande, where a water-powered mill was built, in 1878. Strikes at Leadville, Colorado, and Tombstone, Arizona, in 1877, the playing out of Virginia City and Bodie mines, and the discoveries at Oro Grande created a fertile environment for renewed exploration of the California desert. Thousands of miners, mechanics, construction workers, laborers, and prospectors fanned out from declining camps, ready to flock to a new bonanza. The Calico Mountains had already received casual examination. When miners directed serious attention toward them, they brought the accumulated experience of the past thirty years.[6]

The immediate inspiration for Lowery Silver's 1881 foray into the Calicos was the development of a group of silver claims, about eight miles west. These were the finds of a solitary prospector, grizzled old George Lee, who between 1875 and 1877 often crossed the sage-dotted sweep in search of minerals. Some four miles north of Waterman (now a railroad maintenance point west of Barstow roughly on the site of the old Grapevine Station), Lee struck something. On November 4,1875, he claimed Lee's Quicksilver Mine, and on August 6,1877, he followed with Lee's Lead

Mine, both registered with the Recorder of the local Grapevine Mining District, Ellis J. "Ellie" Miller. Lee later lost his life in an Indian attack at desolate Old Woman Springs, about fifty miles to the southeast. He died without realizing that he had hit a rich deposit of silver.

In 1880, capitalists Robert Whitney Waterman and John L. Porter appeared on the scene, seeking investment opportunities. Ellie Miller's response to their inquiries included a visit with them to Lee's finds. Experienced mine operators, Waterman and Porter immediately recognized their value, re-located them on December 7, and began to make locations all around them. Renamed the Alpha and Omega Silver Mines, the properties quickly won fame. In time the two partners controlled claims covering an area of several square miles and known collectively as the Waterman Mine, one of California's richest silver producers. Within two years, a road connected Grapevine Station with the mine. Twenty miners worked the property, which held lodgings, an office, and "other buildings." The world's leading mining machinery manufacturer, San Francisco's Pacific Iron Works, had built and shipped equipment for a ten-stamp mill. Twenty-seven men, working two, twelve-hour shifts, operated the mill around the clock.[7]

Lowery Silver's discoveries were the first result of the interest that stirred on the desert and in the San Bernardino Valley as news of Waterman's and Porter's mine spread. While he was searching for promising mineral outcrops, others were joining in the action. At the end of 1880 San Bernardino County sheriff John C. King became involved, through a conversation in his office with Frank Mecham. Frank, his brother Charles, and their father Lafayette Mecham, who had earlier operated the Camp Cady station and then that at Fish Ponds, were currently boring artesian wells in the San Bernardino Valley. One day when Frank was visiting his office, King asked him if he knew of any mineral showings or veins in the vicinity of Fish Ponds. Mecham recalled a prominent red, iron-capped vein that his father had found years before while looking in the Calicos for an Indian with a stolen horse. After some parleying, Frank, his brother Charles, their uncle Charles "Doc" Yager, and deputies Tom Warden and Hues Thomas agreed to let King grubstake them in return for a share in any discovery.

Before the Mecham group could reach the desert, rival prospectors marked out additional claims in the Calicos. On March 3, 1881, Francisco Archuleta and Oriol Castro struck the Occidental Mine. A few knots of treasure hunters were in the area by the time King's partners arrived on horseback at Grapevine Station in the middle of the month. After securing his advice, they entered into an agreement with Ellie Miller through which they would share in his mining interest and he in any that they developed. They prospected around the Waterman Mine for several days, ranging as far east as the Calicos where, on the 31st, they located the Garfield Mine. On April 1, another party marked the Buckeye and the Red Cloud, following two days later with the Red Jacket. On the fourth Hieronymous Hartman filed on the Silver Hill, and on the fifth, the King Mine. The neighborhood was becoming crowded. Eager silver-seekers were searching the broad valleys, threading the canyons, negotiating narrow and rocky ridges, and crossing steep slopes in growing numbers. Halloos, the sounds of picks and shovels, and hoofbeats echoed across the desert. Multiplying campfires flickered against the dark night sky. A day later, as Frank Mecham recalled in his reminiscences, he and his companions "got an early start for the 'Calico Hills,'" in order to beat competitors. They "found the vein described by his father, and they all got busy putting up location monuments. Within the hour the other parties arrived but they were too late."

It was April 6. High on King Mountain on the east side of Wall Street Canyon the Mechams had found the Silver King, "the wonder of the age . . . the richest and biggest [silver] mine in the state of California." That same day they added the Mammoth Quartz, perhaps a thousand feet to the northwest. On the seventh they followed with the Consolidated and the Lookout. Taking three samples of ore for assays, they rode their mounts across the desert and down the Cajon Pass back to home in San Bernardino. The assays produced disappointing results: the samples tested at $1, $2, and $8 a ton. On April 8, meanwhile, H. M. Barton claimed the Bullion. W. N. Joiner *et al.* erected monuments on the Lone Star on May 16. In June, King's partners were back at work on the Silver King, without much enthusiasm. Then one day at month's end, as Charles Mecham remembered it, he agreed to climb several hundred feet up to a prominent ledge high on King Mountain while Hues Thomas explored a lower portion of the Silver King vein. While advancing upward, he noticed "some little lumps on the rocks which resembled blisters on a fir tree." He began to cut them with his knife, then, with growing eagerness, with his pick. The material was soft and metallic, responding to cutting in the same manner "as a lead bullet." Bright silvery flecks adhered to his knife and pick. Sure that he had struck it rich, he rushed down to Thomas shouting, "Look here. Pure horn silver." After momentary disbelief, his companions joined in the excitement. News of their luck and exhibition of their ore ushered in the era of mining in the Calicos proper.

Numerous important discoveries followed throughout the remainder of

1881. Among them were G. Gilbert's Occidental, September 7; J. W. Taggart's Blackfoot Mine, November 8; and Robert Dougherty's Calico Tunnel, December 30. From August through October in 1882, J. K. Kincaid located twenty-nine claims including the Morning Star, the Evening Star, the Bismarck, and the Birdseye. A. J. Merchant's and G. A. Beeler's optimistically named Comstock followed on October 25. Lowery Silver finally struck it rich when he discovered the Sue on December 15,1883. By then, some three hundred claims had been marked in the Calicos. Perhaps as many as three to four thousand eager, dirty, sweat-drenched seekers of fortune or of just plain work had thronged to the district.[8]

The discoverers of the Calico ores found that the range lay at the eastern end of a nine-miles-wide by eighteen-miles-long mineralized zone that extended west to the Waterman Mine. Gneissic and granitic bedrock, broken by numerous volcanic intrusions, underlay severely contorted metamorphic and alluvial deposits. Silver appeared principally in three areas. The first mines opened, the Silver King, Oriental, and others, lay just north of the site on which the town of Calico developed, "on the steep sides of . . . Wall Street Canyon and on King Mountain." The most common local silver mineral was cerargyrite, a "naturally occurring silver chloride, colloquially called 'horn silver' . . . ." Embolite, a similar mineral, also occurred in the district, but it was much less abundant. Both of these minerals were termed "secondary," because they formed after minerals from original veins dissolved and then were redeposited in fissures near the earth's surface. Their occurrence was in a system of steeply-dipping (75 to 85 degrees) veins ranging in width from "less than a quarter of an inch to perhaps fifty feet" and sometimes "traceable on the surface for many hundreds of feet." A mile or so to the northeast lay the area that came to be known as East Calico. There, mineralization was more diverse, pervasive, and pockety, containing some veins and many stock works of innumerable silver mineral-filled fractures in the rock. Most prominent in the Bismarck, Garfield, Blackfoot, and Occidental Mines, deposits here were very shallow. The third silver mineral zone was associated with the Calico fault, along the southwest flank of the mountains. Here lay the Waterloo Mine, about a mile west of Calico.

Unlike Virginia City, Leadville, or Cripple Creek, Calico's silver was not typically associated with base metals, the sale of which could pay for processing. It was instead surrounded by a gangue (waste matter) of jasper and barite. Local ores were typically at or close to the surface. This was probably the result of their origin through precipitation after mineral-laden waters pushed through fissures to the surface and cooled, according to

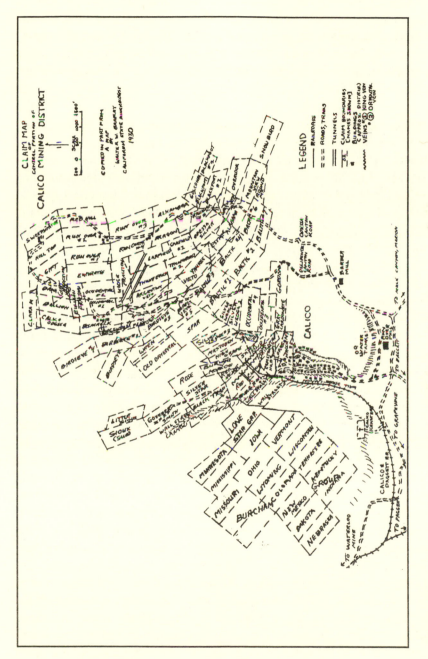

Claim Map, Central Portion of Calico Mining District

Waldemar Lindren, in his classic 1887 report, "The Silver Mines of Calico, California." Where tunneling was necessary, the bedrock was generally strong enough to require virtually no timbering. Easily mined, Calico's most accessible and richest ores averaged from fifty to one hundred ounces of silver per ton, with some two-fist sized chunks of pure silver. The average grade fell off to between ten and twenty ounces as mining proceeded downward.[9]

Initially, mining in the Calicos was extremely crude. The Silver King put eight to ten men, at least one of them with experience in the mines at Ivanpah, to work during the summer of 1881. At first, the crew camped on the floor of Wall Street Canyon. They had to depend on animal and man power to extract and move ore. After digging it out, they "dragged it down" King Mountain's jagged slope "on raw hides, as they proved to be more durable than anything else." Transported by wagon to the railroad, the first carload went to San Francisco, where it turned out to be worth, according to Charles Mecham, between $400 and $500 a ton.

However optimistic early adventurers to Calico might be, difficulties such as those facing developers of the Silver King were typical. At first, brute physical labor was the only means available for wrestling ore out of the ground and to a point where it could be loaded on wagons. Until roads were cut through tortuous Odessa and Occidental Canyons, only human bearers and pack animals could carry ore out of the mountains. Until mills were built locally, ores had to be either crushed on site with primitive arrastres (posts around which chained draft animals dragged heavy stones to pulverize ore for amalgamation of the silver with mercury and then further processing) or freighted to the mill at Oro Grande. The closest two arrastres were at Fish Ponds. The one for which records survive was nine feet in diameter, powered by one horse, and could crush but one-half ton of ore in eight hours.[10] The nearby Waterman Mill, which shipped a $2,000 bar of silver "every few days," could handle little beyond the Waterman Mine's output. By 1882, the Silver King's owners had arranged for the mill in Oro Grande to treat their ores. The wagon haul from Calico to Oro Grande cost $20 per ton of ore, milling another $25. Adding the cost of extraction meant that only material worth $80 or more of silver per ton paid. Less valuable ore piled up on dumps. If the milled ores produced a high-grade concentrate, rather than pure silver, the concentrate was sent to the Selby Smelting Company in San Francisco for final processing. Overcoming these difficulties required large injections of capital, and technology, which were beyond the means of most of the discoverers of the mines. Unless both were forthcoming, mining at Calico faced a bleak future at best.

Drayage to Oro Grande was a demanding enterprise. A round trip required four days. Three corral men cared for animals and maintained wagon camps at Fish Ponds and Stoddard Well. The operation employed 130 mules and 10 drivers (teamsters) and helpers (swampers). Four, twenty-mule rigs, each of a wagon, trailer, and water tanker, were constantly on the trail, clouds of dust and the jingling of bells on the lead animals announcing their progress. But only twenty-five tons of ore a day reached Oro Grande.[11] Calico's output remained quite small, as did the value of local mines through mid 1882. While the Waterman had by then produced $100,000 the Burning Moscow had yielded only $25,000, the Blackfoot $15,000, the Odessa, $9,000. The Silver King's total assessed valuation (including buildings, machinery, and ore on the dump) was only $9,000.

So far, the evidence suggests, there was much more talk of mining than there was actual mining in the neighborhood. Herman F. Mellen later recalled that as a fresh young arrival in September 1882 he was "all ears and eyes, listening to the talk going on among the men in the restaurant" as he consumed his first dinner in the new settlement. To him this talk "sounded as if half the diners were wealthy men to whom a few thousands of dollars were a mere bagatelle." While dinner progressed, "mills and roads were planned, railroads laid out and new camps started as though such things were mere incidents of the day's work. This planning," he drily added, "was done by men mostly with no money at all, or at most enough for a few weeks' living expenses. However, hope ran high." Events of the next two and a half years actually showed, as he recalled it, "how much men of this type could, and did, do with no other capital than strong hands and the will to do." These accomplishments lay in the future, however. For the moment, the chief accompaniment of the talk was an enthusiastic buying and selling—that is, speculating—in real estate in the form of claims.[12]

After mid-1882, Calico mining expanded rapidly, peaking through the mid decade. It is difficult to arrive at a credible estimate of total production. While under its initial ownership, said one partner, the "King mine . . . was very carelessly managed," its records poor. Any engineering reports from the mines, wrote a geologist in the 1960s, "apparently no longer exist." The Director of the Mint in 1886 identified a further difficulty. "The owners and those having charge of producing properties" in San Bernardino County, he wrote, "as a whole are very reticent about the condition or production of their mines," perhaps, we may wonder, because they hoped to sell their mines for speculative gain? Necessarily, the Director had to depend upon

"outside parties" for his information. At that, his information was for the
county, rather than for individual mines.

Given these qualifications, then, one must depend on official estimates for
the county, on such mill records as can be found, and fragmentary material
from the San Francisco Mint and United States Bureau of Mines files. Mill
records show that milling recovered between 75 and 90 percent of Calico's
ores. Ores for the Silver King averaged sixty-four ounces per ton in 1883,
twenty ounces in 1886, and thirty-six ounces for the period 1882 through
1886, according to one early report. Waldemar Lindgren said of the district
that ores there rarely ran below $20 per ton and "often in the hundreds."
The Garfield appears to have averaged about thirty-six ounces a ton in 1886
and 1887, the Waterman about forty-five ounces in 1883. Confidential
manuscript records of the United States Bureau of Mines, and of the San
Francisco Mint where Calico's silver was typically sold, together with local
mill records and annual state reports place San Bernardino County output
in the ranges shown in Table 2.1. Both the mint and the bureau set
production in the Calico district in 1889 at roughly $610,000, or essentially
the county total. The county figure for 1881 to 1899 was on the order of
$15.5 million. Even allowing for the incompleteness of records, Calico's
output, if one includes silver from the Waterman Mine, would be about $14
million to $15 million. In retrospect, this may seem to be a small enough

Table 2.1
San Bernardino County Silver Production, 1881-1900

1881	$ 100,000	1886	$1,204,000	1891	$ 711,151	1896	$ 130,714
1882	150,000	1887	733,268	1892	67,072	1897	54,407
1883	3,706,000	1888	1,200,000	1893	447,000	1898	32,000
1884	2,283,000	1889	824,000	1894	148,243	1899	125,603
1885	2,363,000	1890	795,000	1895	219,410	1900	172,759

Sources: Harold F. Weber, Jr., "Silver Deposits of the Calico District," *Mineral
Information Service*, 20 (Sacramento, February, 1967), 11; annual reports of the Director
of the United States Mint, United States 47 Congress, 1 Sess.-57 Congress, 2 Sess., House
of Representatives *Documents* or *Executive Documents* Nos. [various], "Precious Metals
of the United States . . . 1881-1899 (Washington: Government Printing Office, 1882-
1900); and various yearly reports of the California State Mineralogist, of which see
especially H. T. Cloudman *et al.*, *Report XV of the State Mineralogist* (Sacramento,
1919). J. T. Weakely, for a time owner of both the Silver King and the Waterloo, in a
personal letter to the author, May 8,1958, set the output of those mines alone at $12
million and $9 million respectively through the 1920s.

sum. Placed in the context of the times, it appears differently. The district when it was most productive accounted for more than 10 percent of the nation's annual silver yield in the year 1883.[13]

The arrival of large-scale capital, the consolidation of holdings, and the introduction of modern industrial technology fueled intensive development of Calico's mines. The process began at the Waterman Mine. The Waterman's progress also illustrated Calico's participation in national economic trends. Prominent among these were a growing role for corporations, the concentration of ownership and of political with economic power and multiplying connections with the larger world of commerce through the import of investment funds, supplies, and machinery; and the export of silver for sale in a globally shaped market. Robert Waterman grew up in Sycamore, Illinois. He rushed to California in 1850, returned to the Prairie State and helped form the Republican Party, and moved permanently to California in 1874. His namesake mine yielded $1.7 million before it closed in 1887. He served as governor, from 1887 to 1891.

As early as August, 1882, the *Los Angeles Times* reported that "Negotiations" had "been going on for some time for the sale of the [Silver] King mine at Calico to San Francisco capitalists," for an asking price of $300,000. An assayer "reported that while it was a good mine, it was not worth the money asked." The original owners sold the property that October to Henry Harrison Markham for a price variously reported at $60,000 to $300,000. At either figure, the deal was a bargain. The mine offered up at least $2.5 million in silver before 1900. Markham was a native of New England. After serving in the Civil War, he amassed a fortune as an attorney in Milwaukee. He relocated in 1879 to Pasadena for reasons of health and grew even wealthier. He served as Republican Congressman, from 1883 to 1885, and later succeeded Waterman as governor. His purchase marked the entry of important Milwaukee capital interests into Calico. Democrat John Daggett, an 1862 migrant from New York to California, made his fortune in mining in the northern region of the state. Although never actually a local resident, "from [1881] . . . until 1885 he operated" the Odessa Mining Company "in the Calico District. . . ." New Englander John Sanborn Doe had come to San Francisco in 1852 and entered the lumber and construction businesses. He also came to hold extensive mining interests. The most notable at Calico were the Run Over and Garfield Mines. A widely respected man "of acumen and integrity," Doe died in 1894, "leaving a large estate."[14]

Behind these and other transactions stood a crucial fact. Local needs for capital brought the age of the corporation and consolidation to Calico as

early as 1882. On June 12, Markham, said to be an agent for Milwaukee
investors in other ventures, joined with William Clancy, Edward P. Johnson,
J. F. Crank, A. H. Judson, D. R. Risky, and C. H. Watts, all of Los Angeles
or Pasadena, to form the Calico Union Mining Company, capitalized at a
nominal $900,000 on an issue of ninety thousand shares subscribed by the
seven directors. Through this firm, Markham acquired the Silver King that
October. The details are murky, but the affairs of this company and those
of the Oro Grande, in which Milwaukee interests were important, soon
converged. In 1883, it purchased the Oriental Mill, extending its holdings
and advancing concentration of ownership in the district.[15] Meanwhile, on
April 23,1882, John Daggett, who then listed Calico as his residence, and
four San Franciscans incorporated the Alhambra Consolidated Mining
Company, with a modest subscription of $2,500 in stock. By 1884, it
controlled a large group of claims in East Calico centering on the Bismarck,
Odessa, Alhambra, and others.[16]

Two years later, on March 18,1885, nine Calico businessmen formed the
Calico Water Works Company, capitalized at $40,000. On July 13,1885,
Valentine Blatz and two associates from Milwaukee, with two from Daggett,
incorporated the Calico Mining and Reduction Company with an initial
stock subscription of $30,000. That same year, Waterman and John L.
Porter acquired the Sue.[17] Five San Bernardinans incorporated the Calico
Consolidated Mining Company on April 20,1886, with an initial
subscription of $180,000. In 1888, the Waterloo, another important
discovery from Calico's early years, through merger with the Calico Union
became successor to the Oro Grande's claims.[18] That same year the
company's holdings passed to the Silver King Mining Company,
Limited—incorporated by seven investors in London, England on April 12.
Three years later, this firm bought from John S. Doe all of his Garfield/Run
Over company's claims for £350,000, of which £30,000 was paid in cash
and the rest could be paid in stock nominally valued at £1 per share. The
purchasers never met their cash obligations. The seller and his attorney
appear to have been the only beneficiaries of the transaction. They may
have sold as many as sixty thousand of their shares before the company,
which frittered its $31,000 profit of 1893 on a feckless gold mining venture,
was dissolved in 1899.[19]

It is time to turn back to the development of the Calico mines. A roaring,
roiling, muddy, rock-laden spring flood drove the first arrivals from the
bottom of Wall Street Canyon. They relocated on a narrow bench
immediately to the east, extending south below King Mountain and bounded

on the east by a gully. It was here that Calico took shape as a town, along a single street. The settlement passed a milestone in May 1882, when optimistic residents met and formed the Calico Mining District. Separated from the Grapevine Mining District, the new entity was ten miles square. Commencing at a small butte about two and one-half miles southwest of Calico, its boundaries comprehended township 11 north, range 1 east, the west half of township 11 north, range 2 east, the northern two-thirds of township 10 north, range 1 east, and the northern two-thirds of the west half of township 10 north, range 2 east of the San Bernardino Baseline and Meridian. Fortunately, the *Calico Print* published the district's by-laws, which took effect on June 10. If it had not, it is unlikely that their text would have survived, for one of the fires that swept through Calico consumed all of the district's records. The by-laws were as revealing in their omissions as they were in their contents. They provided for the marking and registration of claims as specified in the federal Mining Law of 1872, set a registration fee, and prescribed the annual election of a single officer, a Recorder. Individuals could locate multiple claims, each of roughly twenty acres, measuring fifteen hundred feet long with side boundaries set three hundred feet back on each side of the apex of a vein. Since the federal statute prescribed the annual assessment work necessary to retain a claim, the by-laws did not refer to the value of such activity. They also contained no provisions to enforce claim rights or the law, since state and county law enforcement prevailed from the beginning. Unlike frontier predecessors, Calico was within the reach of government and the law from its origin. It could scarcely have been otherwise with the sheriff of a well-established county among the earliest local mine owners.

It turned out to be no easier in Calico than elsewhere to determine who had priority of right, where the apex of a vein was (given the tendency of veins to outcrop at more than one spot and to dip, or incline erratically from their longitudinal axes, and strike, or veer in varying degree, from their horizontal axes), and whether claims had been properly marked. The results were predictable. They included at least three major law suits and one countersuit. All pitted John S. Doe against the owners of the Silver King. All centered on disputed mining rights on the richest portion of King Mountain. All originated in the San Bernardino County Superior Court. All were tried, on petition of the defendants, in the Ninth United States Circuit Court, Southern District of California, since the litigants were either individual or corporate citizens of different states, California and Wisconsin. Two originated in disputes over the boundaries of the Mammoth Quartz, which overlapped to the east with the Red Jacket and to the west with the

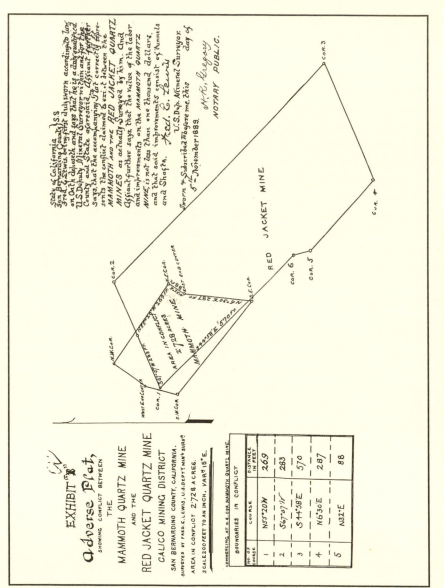

Map, Adverse Plat, Mammoth Quartz and Red Jacket Mines

Josephine. Doe won control of the Mammoth Quartz in August 1884, when he bought the Oriental Mining and Milling Company.

The first controversy erupted in August 1889, when the owners of the Waterloo Mining Company attempted to patent the Josephine, recording its boundaries so as to include part of the Mammoth Quartz. Doe gave notice of an adverse claim and filed suit. Three months later, when the Waterloo sought to patent the Red Jacket bounded so that it, too, would incorporate parts of the Mammoth Quartz, Doe protested and filed a second suit. The disputed area in this case was about 2.7 acres. The court did not render a decision until April 1893. When it did, it found for Doe in the case of the Josephine, and against him in that of the Red Jacket. The discovery of the Red Jacket on April 3, 1881, it held, antedated that of the Mammoth Quartz. Although the locator of the Red Jacket had erected but a single monument in its center, he had attached to the monument a notice describing the claim's boundaries and stating his intention to place the necessary markers along its axis and perimeter within twenty days. The locators of the Mammoth Quartz had erred in disregarding this plainly visible monument and notice in bounding it so that it overlapped with the Red Jacket.[20]

Just a week before, on March 27, the circuit court had settled the most famous case to originate in Calico. *Doe v. Waterloo Mining Company* was a classic apex suit. At issue was the question whether or not the vein in the Oriental No. 2 was a separate vein, or an extension of the Silver King vein. If the latter were found to be the case, then Doe's miners could follow the vein from the Oriental No. 2 wherever it led meaning, in this instance, into the King claim. After prolonged argument buttressed by testimony from a battery of experts, the owners of the Silver King prevailed. Meanwhile, in 1891 they had sued Doe for $90,000 and costs, for tunneling from the Oriental No. 2 and removing from the Silver King over a period of a year three thousand tons of ore valued at $30 a ton. Doe countersued, alleging that his rivals had dug a drift into the Oriental and taken out ore without his consent. This litigation ended after Doe's death, when his heirs in 1895 agreed to pay a $100,000 out of court settlement.[21]

Not all of the Calico mining disputes ended in court, or so peacefully. A conflict over a rich claim near the Occidental in East Calico produced an armed standoff, which did not end in a shootout only because of the timely arrival of local deputy sheriff Joseph Le Cyr.[22] Three of the four owners of the Burning Moscow, as will be seen, engaged in mutual slaughter.[23]

There was money to be made in town planting and development as well as in mining at Calico. On July 5, 1882, the four proprietors, H. McDonald, Joe Brunnel, Nelson Wager, and S. Benjamin had the town site surveyed.

Even that early, building had advanced so far that several structures had to be removed "a few feet from their present location," to place them entirely within the boundaries of their lots. The end of summer's heat in October sped shipments of lumber from San Bernardino and the erection of houses, stores, and other buildings. The Silver King brought in crews to begin working on a trestle and tramway from the mine entrance, a chute, and an ore bin with a capacity of two hundred tons. The men, working without detailed plans, sawed, hammered, nailed, and bolted these facilities together by February 1883. Soon after, surveyors marked a route, and laborers and teams noisily cut and graded a road to the bin at the base of the chute. The trestle extended out from King Mountain to a point ninety feet in the air. At its end, miners tipped ore cars, sending a rumbling cascade of rock down a 1,500-foot chute, angled at 32 degrees, to the bin far below. Straining mule teams drew lumbering, noisy freight wagons up to the bin for loading, then to the mill for processing.

Similar tramways, trestles, chutes, and bins permitted large-scale mining at the Bismarck, Odessa Silver, Alabama, Oriental, and other mines in short order. Before workers carved roads into Wall Street, Odessa, Occidental, and other canyons allowing the use of teams and wagons to bring in lumber, burro pack trains were the only practical means of getting it to mine construction sites. Packers seated astride horses used lead lines to guide the trains through the narrow, labyrinthine defiles. Each burro bent low beneath four, two-by-twelve-inch-by-sixteen-foot timbers, or two, eight-by-ten-inch-by-sixteen-foot pieces. Teamsters placed "timbers on each side of the burro crossing them above the burro's head with the rear ends dragging the ground." Carpenters fashioned a wooden platform high in Odessa Canyon where the new trail ended, at the ore bin of the Odessa Mine. There, arriving teams were unhitched. Workmen skidded the wagons around to face downhill, so that the animals could be rehitched and the rigs could be driven back down on the return trip.[24]

The mines themselves took two main forms. Because the richest ores were closest to the surface, even many veins such as that of the Silver King could be reached by driving a series of drifts (horizontal tunnels along veins) into mountain sides at different elevations, rather than by digging shafts and taking recourse to hoisting machinery. The King was ultimately worked at nine different levels, and it did use at least one whim (animal-powered winch) to raise buckets of ore. Some other mines, such as the Red Jacket and the Garfield, were worked at as many as five or more levels. Several mines' tunnels totaled 4,000 feet or more and reached depths of 500 feet. Occasionally, timbering was necessary in stopes (large excavated rooms in the mines). In East Calico, with its stockworks and pockety deposits, miners could grub ore from the surface itself. The Humbug was worked as a quarry, about 300-by-300 feet and 30 feet deep. Nearby properties were managed similarly. Where deposits were too small to interest larger operators, individuals or small groups could hope to prosper, at least temporarily, by gophering into the slopes. Whether dug underground or at the surface, the ores underwent an initial screening to capture the richest particles of silver. Afterward, workers sorted the coarser material by hand. They muscled the valuable matter in metal ore cars along rails for dumping down chutes to ore bins. The work proceeded as rapidly as human ingenuity and energy allowed. When summer's withering heat blasted the desert and transformed distant valleys, hills, and peaks into indistinct, shimmering images, the pace of outdoor labor slowed almost to a standstill. When the weather again became more bearable, it picked up.

Miners called Calico's ores "docile." The term meant that they were easily processed. Rapidly expanding production quickly outran the capacity of the Waterman and Oro Grande mills. By 1883, the Oriental Mining Company operated a ten-stamp mill at Daggett. A five-stamp mill was open at Hawley's Station, eight miles east of Calico on the Mojave River. The Silver King had erected a two-stamp mill. Within another five years, some 187 stamps thudded an ear-splitting din in local mills. The Oriental Mill had passed to the Silver King and had expanded to fifteen, twenty, then thirty stamps by 1889. Barber's Mill in West Calico drove ten stamps. The Daggett Sampling Works ran five. In 1888 the Waterloo built a $250,000, sixty-stamp, electrically lit facility just north of Daggett at Elephant Butte. A year later the company laid down a narrow gauge railroad connecting the mill to its mine and to Calico, along a route paralleling the telephone line to the settlement. The coming of the railroad meant that it now cost but twelve cents a ton to get ore from the mine to the mill. Area mills still charged $25 to $30 per ton of ore for custom milling. The actual cost of milling ran between $3.10 and $4.60. The total production cost, with miners' daily pay beginning at $4.00 and settling by the late 1880s to $3.00, was perhaps $10.45 per ton. This translated into roughly fifty to sixty cents per ounce of silver.[25]

All of the new mills reflected W. P. Boss's improvements on the Washoe pan process that Almarin B. Paul had devised in 1860 to treat the rich ores of Virginia City, Nevada. Collectively they were emblematic, with the railroad, telegraph, telephone, and electric lighting at the Waterloo Mill, of the triumph locally of modern industrial technology. A detailed description survives for the Garfield/Run Over Mill. Set between the openings of Wall

Miners, Ore Train, Calico & Daggett Rail Road at Silver King Mine. *Photo courtesy Mojave River Valley Museum.*

Silver King (also known as Garfield) Mill. *Photo courtesy Mojave River Valley Museum.*

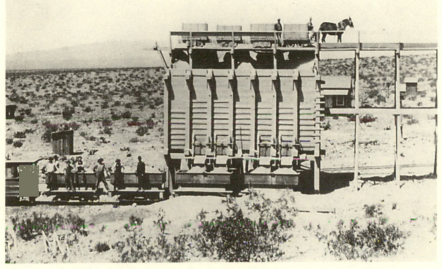

Waterloo Mine Ore Bin at Calico & Daggett R. R. Note mules backed to bin. *Photo courtesy Mojave River Valley Museum.*

Waterloo Mine Ore Train, Calico & Daggett R. R. *Photo courtesy Mojave River Valley Museum.*

Waterloo Mill Toward Calico Peak (behind flagpole). Note workers' cottages. *Photo courtesy Mojave River Valley Museum.*

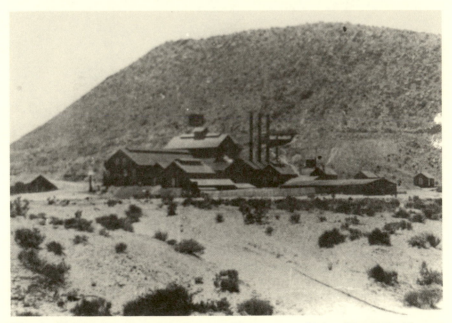

Waterloo Mill. Elephant Butte in background. *Photo courtesy Mojave River Valley Museum.*

General View, Upper Calico Street, ca. 1890. *Photo courtesy Mojave River Valley Museum.*

Close-up, Upper One-third of Calico Street, ca. 1890. *Photo courtesy Mojave River Valley Museum.*

Street and Odessa Canyons at the edge of the mountains, it was run by shifts of three men. Gravity continuously fed ore from a bin to a battery of twenty, 850-pound stamps. Raised by a revolving crankshaft powered by a smoke-belching steam engine, the thundering stamps dropped eight inches and pulverized the ore. The resulting powder passed to a series of eight, five and a half foot-diameter iron pans, and finally to three settling tanks. The iron pans revolved sixty-five times per minute, driven by bevel gear attachments to a main drive shaft. For each pan there was a clutch, so that pans could be disengaged and repaired without idling the entire mill. Quicksilver was added to water and pulverized ore in the first pan, an iron muller let down, and the mixture finely ground and stirred together, to allow the mercury and silver to amalgamate as an alloy. The sludge underwent more mulling in a second pan, then flowed to a third where copper sulphate and sodium chloride and more quicksilver were added to further the process of amalgamation. The pulp passed through a fourth pan and into a fifth, where caustic lime was introduced to clear the quicksilver. The remaining mixture, water washing away lighter particles of gangue, flowed to settling tanks, eight feet in diameter and revolving twenty times per minute. The resulting concentrate was either heated in a retort to drive off and capture the mercury for reuse, leaving pure silver, or smelted as necessary.

The entire process was automatic and self-timed. Gravity and flowing hot water powered a continuous feeder system that moved the ore. A pulpy stream of water and crushed ore entered the first pan through a thirty-mesh screen; material too large to pass through underwent further stamping. The operation consumed two thousand gallons of water per ton of ore. Using a technology that worked "admirably" with Calico's "free processing" ores, the mill recovered from the concentrated amalgam about 95 percent of the purest chloride ores' assay values, and 75 to 80 percent from baser ores, results typical of the most advanced local mills. Calico concentrates went via Wells, Fargo to San Francisco, Nevada, or Colorado for smelting when it was necessary. The Garfield Mill averaged thirty-three tons of ore per day, working around the clock.[26] Coal arrived by rail from New Mexico, supplanting the wood that had long since been cut from the edge of the Mojave River to fuel the voracious local mills. Lumber for such timbering as was required, and for building construction, came after the completion of the Atlantic and Pacific Railroad, in 1883, from the great ponderosa pine forest around Flagstaff, Arizona.[27]

Outside forces cast Calico's fate. Dependent on an extractive industry, as was much of the West, the camp was active at a critical point in the evolution of silver mining and of national monetary policy. An importer of silver until Virginia City and other western towns began to pour out their treasure, the United States became the world's leading producer of the white metal from 1871 to 1915. The relationship between the price of gold, at about $22.00 per ounce, and silver, long around $1.32 an ounce, changed as silver prices began to decline under the weight of rising output. Annual silver production mounted from 12.4 million to 28.9 million ounces, between 1870 and 1874, fell briefly in 1875, and then shot to 63 million ounces in 1892.

Meanwhile, in February 1873, monetary conservatives pushed through Congress the Coinage Act, ending the coinage of silver dollars. In 1875 they added the Specie Resumption Act, requiring the Treasury to begin payments in gold alone on January 1,1879, and reducing federal paper currency circulation by about 20 percent. These measures and a severe business depression that struck in 1873 battered silver prices further. Western interests won some relief when Congress in 1878 passed the Bland-Allison Act over a presidential veto. The law obliged the Treasury to buy $2 million to $4 million in silver each month. It bought only the minimum amount prescribed. By 1881, when discoveries began in the Calico area, the average price of silver had fallen to $1.11. It dipped to $1.06 in 1885, and fell below $1.00 in 1886. The admission to the Union of six new Western states in 1889 and 1890 and Congressional dealing over a Republican proposal to raise the tariff brought temporary succor in 1890 in the form of the Sherman Silver Purchase Act. This law compelled the Treasury to buy at market prices 4.5 million ounces of silver a month, essentially the nation's entire output. It was to pay for the silver with new paper notes—called silver certificates—redeemable in either gold or silver at the option of the Treasury, and to coin the silver. Silver prices briefly recovered to $1.04 in 1890, but the chief effect of the measure was to inspire panic among monetary conservatives. They redeemed their silver certificates in gold and thus began an erosion of the Treasury gold reserve that raised the specter of its exhaustion and a resulting abandonment of a gold standard of payment.[28]

Even with a relatively low cost of production after the completion of a railroad and modern new mills in the vicinity, the progressive exhaustion of richer deposits and the falling value of local ores made it unprofitable to mine at Calico when silver prices fell below a dollar. Declining silver prices "resulted disastrously." Although conditions occasionally held out hope for improvement, for three years after 1888 annual production hovered disappointingly between $711,000 and $824,000, less than 20 percent of the 1883 level. It plummeted afterward. Calico's population fluctuated with silver prices and mining activity. In 1890 alone it may have ranged between about four hundred and a thousand.

Financial panic announced the arrival of a catastrophic business depression in May 1893. Early that summer, President Grover Cleveland summoned Congress into special session to repeal the Sherman Act and relieve the fears of fiscal conservatives as to the safety of the gold standard. After weeks of bitter wrangling, stubborn congressional defenders of silver went down in defeat, and repeal came on October 30. Meanwhile, the British government had announced the end of the coinage of silver in India, previously a major silver consumer. The impact on silver markets was devastating. Silver prices collapsed to an average of $0.63 in 1894. The stage was set for the climactic presidential election of 1896, when fervent advocates of the unlimited coinage of silver at its historic value/weight ratio of 16:1 with gold followed William Jennings Bryan in his resoundingly unsuccessful campaign against Republican William McKinley and the gold standard.[29] By one account, Calico's remaining residents snubbed its only two openly avowed Republicans. "Huddled around the telegraph" at the general store of John R. and Lucy Lane, they learned of McKinley's triumph and felt their hopes begin to drain away.

The Waterloo, Garfield, and Odessa Mines all closed for the last time in 1896. That same year, fire destroyed the Barber Mill. After the election, according to Lucy Lane, many of the miners "left as soon as possible . . .and Mr. Lane fed their families until they could earn money to send for them." As happened in many camps in the mining West, where lumber was scarce and machinery difficult and expensive to come by, many of Calico's mining and mill structures were dismantled for scrap and reuse elsewhere. After the turn of the century, the mill trestles, bins, and railroad connections of the Silver King suffered this fate. A number of houses were relocated to Yermo or Daggett, where they still stand. In 1900, twenty-five voters still cast ballots in Calico. There were still a good many more residents than that, and the desert never completely reclaimed the town. Desultory attempts to work tailings and ore dumps continued from time to time. "Chloriders," individuals or small groups of miners leasing portions of claims for 20 to 25 percent of their earnings, accounted for most of the activity. As late as the 1930s, there were efforts to renew mining. Calico's glory days as a silver camp were over, though. Decaying ore bins, chutes and trestles, heaps of trash and mounds of tailings, and fading trails and railroad rights of way commemorated its brief and representative chapter in the story of the exploitation of western resources. It was ironic and characteristic that in chasing the chimera of quick mineral wealth the people of Calico used up the very resource on which their livelihoods and dreams depended, and in doing so added to the swelling output that reduced its value. Their tale resembled that of hundreds of mining camps, remote outliers of the larger, industrializing national economy.[30]

Old Calico was not quite through, however. It had one more card to play. That card turned out to be an ace. In playing it, Calico managed to survive one more hand in the high stakes poker game that was the history of Western mining. It also left a much greater mark than it would have if silver had been its only important product.

NOTES

1. "Index to Mines, San Bernardino County" (unpublished record of claims filed in the county since 1855), I-II, in San Bernardino County Archives. Listings are by date and by surname of claimant; pages are not numbered.

2. For background, David Williams, *The Georgia Gold Rush: Twenty-Niners, Cherokees, and Gold Fever* (Columbia: University of South Carolina Press, 1993) is the new standard work on its subject, and its bibliography is exhaustive for the Southeastern rush of the 1830s. Also Rodman Wilson Paul, *California Gold: The Beginning of Mining in the Far West* (Cambridge: Harvard University Press, 1947), 48; Paul, *Mining Frontiers of the Far West, 1848-1880* (New York: Harper & Row Publishers, 1963), 3-7, 19, 37-48, 113-14; and Paul, *The Far West and the Great Plains in Transition, 1859-1890* (New York: Harper & Row Publishers, 1988), 24-91, 252-82; Duane A. Smith, *Rocky Mountain West: Colorado, Wyoming, and Montana, 1859-1915* (Albuquerque: University of New Mexico Press, 1992), 18-19, 36-37, 52-53, 82-84; and, a synthesis of recent work, Richard White, *"It's Your Misfortune and None of My Own": A History of the American West* (Norman: University of Oklahoma Press, 1991), 191-92, 223-24, 280-90.

3. United States Code, 1958, 6 (Washington, 1958), 5,484-5,487, Title 30, Chapter 2, Sections 22-29; Charles Howard Shinn, *Land Laws of Mining Districts* (Baltimore: Johns Hopkins University Press, 1884), 7ff; Paul, *Far West*, 258-59, 261; Smith, *Rocky Mountain West*, 72-74; A. H. Ricketts, *American Mining Law, with Forms and Precedents*, 4th Edition, 2 volumes (Sacramento: California Division of Mines, 1948).

4. *Calico Print*, July 27, 1882, also July 8, 20, 1882. Further information, Virgie Timmons, "Early Days in Daggett" (unpublished manuscript, Daggett, 1949, in author's possession); H. L. Waters, *Steel Trails to Santa Fe* (Lawrence: University of Kansas Press, 1950), 70-74, 340-43; [Anonymous], *Historical Outline: Southern Pacific Company* (San Francisco: Bureau of News, Development Department, Southern Pacific Company, 1931), 42-43; [Anonymous], *History of San Bernardino County, California, With Illustrations* . . . (San Francisco: Wallace W. Elliot & Co., Publishers, 1883), 75-76.

5. Eliot Lord, *Comstock Mining and Miners*. A Reprint of the 1883 Edition. With an Introduction by David F. Myrick (Berkeley: Howell-North, 1959); Paul, *Mining Frontiers*, 31-33, 56-86.

6. Paul, *Mining Frontiers*; Smith, *Rocky Mountain West*. Popular accounts, Remi Nadeau, *Ghost Towns and Mining Camps of California* (Los Angeles: The Ward Ritchie Press, 1965), esp. 187-209, 239-260ff; and Muriel Sibell Wolle, *The Bonanza Trail: Ghost Towns and Mining Camps of the West* (Bloomington: Indiana University Press, 1953).

7. "Index to Mines," I; [Anonymous], *San Bernardino County*, quoted, 56.

8. Quotations, Frank Mecham, "Reminiscences," in *San Bernardino Sun-Telegram*, May 15, 1938; *Calico Print* in [Anonymous], *San Bernardino County*, 128; Charles Mecham, "Reminiscences," [written about 1920], *San Bernardino Sun-Telegram*, October 26, 1952; claims in "Index to Mines," I, II.

9. Quotations, F. Harold Weber, Jr., "Silver Mining in Old Calico," *Mineral Information Service*, 19 (Sacramento, May, 1966), 74; Weber, "Silver Deposits of the Calico District," *Mineral Information Service*, 20 (Sacramento, February, 1967), 11 and (January, 1967), 8; and Weber, "Economic Geology of the Calico District, California," preprint of paper presented at Society of Mining Engineers Fall Meeting, Rocky Mountain Minerals Conference, Las Vegas, Nevada, September 6-8, 1967, 3-4; Waldemar Lindgren, "The Silver Mines of Calico, California," *Transactions of the American Institute of Mining Engineers*, 15 (May, 1886-February, 1887), 717-34.

10. *Calico Print*, August 3, 1882.

11. *Calico Print*, July 27, see also July 8, August 3, 1882; [Anonymous] *San Bernardino County*, 56; Herman F. Mellen, "Reminiscences of Old Calico," *Historical Society of Southern California Quarterly*, 34 (June, September, December, 1952), 107-24, 243-60, 347-64; John A. Delameter, "My Forty Years Hauling Freight," *Touring Topics*, 22 (August, 1930), 24-25.

12. Mellen, "Reminiscences," (June, 1952), quoted, 114.

13. Quotation, Charles Mecham, "Reminiscences"; Weber, "Silver Deposits," 11; United States, 49 Congress, 2 Sess., House of Representatives, *Executive Document* No. 200, "Precious Metals of the United States, 1886," (Washington: Government Printing Office, 1887), 161. It is maddeningly difficult—for some years figures diverge by 50 percent while for others they are roughly equal—to reconcile the confidential records of the San Francisco Mint and the Bureau of Mines (unpublished manuscripts, copies in author's possession) with the published reports of the Director of the United States Mint, United States 47 Congress, 1 Sess.-United States 57 Congress, 2 Sess., House of Representatives, *Documents* or *Executive Documents* Nos. [various], "Precious Metals of the United States . . . 1881-1899," (Washington: Government Printing Office, 1882-1900); and the various yearly reports of the California State Mineralogist, of which see especially H. T. Cloudman *et al.*, *Report XV of the State Mineralogist* (Sacramento, 1919). Cloudman set total county output, 1881-1913, at $13.8 million, but county records were incomplete for the years before 1900. J. T. Weakely, who for a time owned both the Silver King and the Waterloo and their records, in a personal letter to the author, May 8, 1958, wrote that through the 1920s these mines had yielded $12 million and $9 million respectively.

14. Quotations, *Los Angeles Times* August 18, 1882; Leslie Daggett Hyde, "John Daggett," *D. A. R. Records of the Families of California Pioneers*, 19 (unpublished manuscript, Sacramento, 1949), 60-61; for John Doe, *San Francisco Bulletin*, January 22, 1894. For the sale of the Silver King, also *Calico Print*, October 21,1882. Frank Mecham, "Reminiscences," remembered that Markham took an option on the claim for $150,000 and paid the original owners $25,000 apiece with proceeds from the ore recovered. Charles Mecham, "Reminiscences," said that the sale price for the Silver King was $60,000. Weber, "Silver Mining," 75, following [Anonymous], "San Bernardino," *Mining and Scientific Press*, 45 (July 1, 1882), 2, erroneously set the sale at $300,000, but he also grossly underestimated the local population of mid-1882. See Chapter 5.

15. Articles of Incorporation in San Bernardino County Archives. See also *Calico Print*, July 20, 1882; and Weber, "Silver Mining," 76-77; United States 48 Congress, 2 Sess., House of Representatives, *Executive Document* No. 268 (Washington: Government Printing Office, 1884), 139-40; for the Oro Grande's control of the Silver King, "San Bernardino," *Mining and Scientific Press*, 49 (October 18, 1884), quoting from the *Calico Print*.

16. [Anonymous], "San Bernardino," *Mining and Scientific Press*, 50 (February 21, 1885), quoting the *Calico Print*, February 15, 1885.

17. Articles of Incorporation, San Bernardino County Archives; consolidation, William Irelan, Jr., *Eighth Annual Report of the State Mineralogist* (Sacramento: State of California, 1888), 491-97.

18. Irelan, *Eighth Report*, 491-97.

19. Records of Silver King Mining Company, Limited, Register of Companies Office, Bush House, London [England], Folder 26328, "Silver King Mining Company, Limited"; microfilm at Bancroft Library, University of California, Berkeley, Microfilm H/F Z G1 GB. Board of Trade. Arch of the Companies Regs Office, Film Z-GL, Reel 3, Part 3.

20. For the by-laws, *Calico Print*, July 8, 1882. See also J. J. Crawford, *Twelfth Annual Report of the State Mineralogist* (Sacramento: State of California, 1894), 376. For the Josephine, *John S. Doe v. Waterloo Mining Company*, 2647 Superior Court, County of San Bernardino (23 August, 1889), the Red Jacket, *John S. Doe v. Waterloo Mining Company*, 2812 Superior Court (1889), both San Bernardino County Archives; and, respectively, *Doe v. Waterloo Mining Company* and *Same v. Same*, Circuit Court, S. D. California, 55 *Federal Reports* (April 3,1893), 11-15.

21. The initial award was for $300,000. In 1895, after Doe's death, the parties settled out of court for $100,000. Apex suit, *Doe v. Waterloo Mining Company*, Circuit Court, S. D., California, 54 *Federal Reports* (March 27, 1893), 935-51. Also Supplementary Agreement of February 24,1891, between John S. Doe and the Silver King Mining Company, Ltd., contained in the records cited in n. 19, above. *Oro Grande Mining Company v. John S. Doe*, 3711 Superior Court, County of San Bernardino (January 20,1891), *John S. Doe v. Oro Grande Mining Company et al.* (1891), "Stipulations Dismissing Action" in same, dated respectively February 28 and February 27,1895; all in San Bernardino County Archives. Protection of mine buildings figured in litigation over the Oregon No. 3. The Circuit Court ruled in that case that neither party had a valid claim because no vein or lode had been discovered. See *Waterloo Mining Company v. Doe et al.*, Circuit Court, S. D. California, 56 *Federal Reports* (April 18, 1893), 685-90. Lucy Bell Lane, *Calico Memories of . . .*, ed. by Alan Baltazar (Barstow: Alan Baltazar, 1993), 7, gave additional information. She knew Doe's attorney.

22. *Calico Print*, February 8, 1885.

23. For the Burning Moscow, *Calico Print*, July 8, 1882, and Chapter 5.

24. "General," *Mining and Scientific Press*, 46 (February 17, 1883), 109, for the chute; (May 10, 1883), 341, for construction of a road up Wall Street Canyon to the Mammoth Quartz Mine and a 600-foot tramway and track below its lower level for it; for Odessa Canyon, (March 17, 1883), 181, and Mellen, "Reminiscences," 116-18, 244.

25. Mining, Lindgren, "Silver Mines"; construction, Mellen, "Reminiscences," 116-18; Irelan, *Eighth Report*, 494-96; James H. Crossman, "San Bernardino County," *Ninth Annual Report of the State Mineralogist* (Sacramento: State of California, 1890), 238; Henry De Groot, "San Bernardino County . . .," *Tenth . . . Report . . .* (Sacramento: State of California, 1890), 518-33; and Weber, "Silver Mining," 76-77; "San Bernardino,"

Mining and Scientific Press, 54 (March 19,1887), 192. Town site survey, *Calico Print*, July 8,1882. The town plat map is in the San Bernardino County Archives.

26. Paul, *Mining Frontiers*, and Lord, *Comstock*, 86-87 for stamp mills.

27. Milling, Lindgren, "Silver Mines," 731-34; Irelan, *Eighth Report*, 491-96; United States, 50 Congress, 1 Sess., House of Representatives, *Executive Document* No. 405 (Washington: Government Printing Office, 1887), 141-47.

28. United States, Bureau of the Census, *Historical Statistics of the United States: Colonial Times to 1957* (Washington: Government Printing Office, 1960), 371. Background, Milton Friedman and Anna Jacobson Schwartz, *A Monetary History of the United States, 1867-1960* (Princeton: Princeton University Press, 1963); Weber, "Silver Mining," 71; Rendigs Fels, *American Business Cycles, 1865-97* (Chapel Hill: University of North Carolina Press, 1959).

29. Fels, *Cycles*, 184-90, 212-13; Friedman and Schwartz, *Monetary History*, 89-113; Charles Hoffmann, *The Depression of the Nineties—An Economic History* (Westport, CT: Greenwood Press, 1970); chloriders, Irelan, *Eighth Report*, 490; W. H. Storms, *Eleventh Report* . . . (Sacramento: State of California, 1893), 344-45, quoted 344; J. J. Crawford, *Twelfth Annual Report* . . . (Sacramento: State of California, 1894), 376 and *Thirteenth Annual Report* . . . (Sacramento: State of California, 1896), 606, 608. Population, mining costs, De Groot, *Tenth . . . Report . . .*, 531, 518-33; Department of the Interior, Census Office, *Compendium of the Eleventh Census: 1890. Part I.—Population*, 3 (Washington: Government Printing Office, 1892), 71.

30. Quotation, salvage, Lucy Lane, personal letter to the author, May 9, 1958. For mine closures, Lauren A. Wright *et al.*, "Mines and Mineral Deposits of San Bernardino County, California," *California Journal of Mines and Geology*, 49 (January-April, 1953), 129-32; Weber, "Silver Mines," 72-76; Barber Mill fire, *San Francisco Chronicle*, May 31, 1896.

Chapter 3

HUGH STEVENS' BEAUTIFUL WHITE CRYSTALS

considerable excitement in Calico District over recent discoveries of borax. . . .
Calico Print, 1883

The Mojave Desert, like the mining West, was a land of illusions. Lakes that gleamed like polished silver in the midsummer heat turned out to be mirages. Patches of green often proved to grow around bitter alkaline springs. Mountains whose outlines shimmered beguilingly in the sweltering summer heat, promising cool relief, receded as travelers approached them. What had seemed to be close was far away, often more than a hundred miles. Rains that evaporated before reaching the ground were a natural part of such a place. Sometimes it was hard to separate fantasy from reality.

The most seductive illusion of all was the dream of finding mineral bonanzas. It propelled those migrating thousands of miners across the desert West during the generation that ended around 1900. It prompted one great rush after another. All too often, the "color" played out quickly, leaving as its legacy disappointment and one more crumbling, deserted ghost camp. And perhaps stories. Stories that were the oral counterpart of the landscape, mixing reality and illusion, fact and fable. Stories of finds. Of jumping frogs. Of—and this was a favorite genre—con men gulling unsuspecting greenhorns into buying salted, worthless claims. They then exited safe in the knowledge that their victims were likely to remain silent out of embarrassment, or to attempt to "try to sell the claim to some other sucker."

Calico was the source of one such story. As the account goes, early in

1883 Hugh Barrett Stevens, a greenhorn from Texas, unwittingly bought a salted silver mine. After a disappointing local examination he sent "his worthless outcroppings to San Francisco for further assaying." The word came back that he had struck a fortune, an outcome that could renew ones faith in poetic justice. His fortune was not in silver, however. It was, like the greater part of all wealth created by mining in the United States, derived from an unglamorous industrial mineral. It was in borax.[1]

The truth is more interesting than the fable about the discovery of Stevens' mine. Although the 1906 San Francisco fire consumed the records of the industry's giant, the Pacific Coast Borax Company, there is ample evidence concerning the story of borax at Calico. Local ores did first win public notice early in 1883, when the *Calico Print* reported "considerable excitement in Calico District over recent discoveries of borax within a couple of miles" of Calico. The "principal deposits," the *Print* continued, lay in the "eastern part of the district" and comprised "an area of four or five miles square. Several sales were made last week of borax claims amounting to $4,250, and since then lands hitherto supposed to be worthless have been located in 20 acre claims as borax deposits." Stevens was no greenhorn. He came to Calico from Pioche, Nevada, and with mining experience. One of Calico's earliest arrivals, he was a well-known storekeeper. He was also an active prospector who located a number of silver claims in the district while living there. In the winter of 1882-1883 he "had decided to extend his prospecting farther east in the Calico Mountains." He did not purchase supposedly worthless silver claims that turned out to be rich in borax. He discovered the deposits himself. There was nothing accidental, nor serendipitous about his decision to send samples to San Francisco for assaying after he struck outcroppings of beautiful, white, crystalline rock in Mule Canyon.[2]

Thomas Price, a San Francisco chemist, assayed the ore for Stevens. He found its composition to be the same as that of Death Valley ore he had recently inspected for William Tell Coleman. Prominent in the vigilante movement of the 1850s and a leading bay area commission merchant, Coleman held extensive and varied interests, and numerous contacts in New York and elsewhere in the East. A decade earlier, in 1872, he had acquired borax properties at Columbus Marsh, Nevada. He later added holdings near Death Valley. Price divulged the new assay results to him before doing so to his client. Coleman at once recognized the promise of the "rich and abundant" Calico ores. His Death Valley operations were 165 miles from the nearest railroads, at Mojave Station and Daggett. The Calico deposits lay but a dozen miles from Daggett. Coleman sent his son-in-law, William

Robertson, to Calico to gain control of the borax claims there. As Lucy Lane recalled in her memoirs, Robertson arrived in town as a stranger one day in 1883. After examining ore samples in a local store, he "quietly bought up the properties for prices far below those asked for silver claims . . . . " Then, "before the population of Calico were aware of what had happened, every parcel with this mineral of doubtful value was owned by one man." Stevens realized $4,500 for his Consolidated Borate Mine Locations Nos. 1, 2, and 3. Not more than $20,000 changed hands for the purchase of all twenty-eight claims in Mule Canyon.[3]

The Calico ores presented novel challenges. They differed in both occurrence and in composition from those mined elsewhere in the West. Coleman began the development of his new properties, putting first nine and then twenty-five men to work there. Progress was slow, the scale of operations small. The first building erected on a Mule Canyon claim, in June, 1883, was only fourteen by forty feet.[4] While awaiting the solution to processing problems, Coleman continued to exploit his Harmony and Amargosa works near Death Valley. Calico's annual output was accordingly very limited through 1888, probably not exceeding 250 short tons, or 500,000 pounds, valued at no more than $33,500. This was a fraction of the national output of 5,500 short tons, or 11,000,000 pounds, worth $550,000.[5] Coleman's role as an active participant in the development of the borax industry ended in 1888. He had relied excessively on credit to build his business empire. Efforts to sell his borax properties for $2 million—twice what he had paid for them—failed. He had assets of perhaps $4.5 million. However, lacking cash to address $2 million in liabilities, he assigned his businesses to receivers. He arranged a settlement with his creditors at forty cents on the dollar. A man of honor, he actually paid them off in full before dying in 1893. Meanwhile, his exit from the borax industry cleared the way for a colossus to enter the scene in the Calicos.[6] Francis Marion "Borax" Smith was to be indelibly associated with the Calico mines.

The youngest son of a Wisconsin farm couple, Smith upon reaching his majority in 1867 had set out for the West, with $155. For several years he drifted around mining camps, washing dishes, running tent restaurants, prospecting, supplying wood to camps in Esmeralda County, Nevada, by means of pack trains. In 1871, observing borax operations at Columbus Marsh, Nevada, he recalled that he had seen another alkali flat about twenty miles distant that looked similar. It was Teel's Marsh. An assay confirmed his hopes. Smith misled the assayer as to the location from which he had taken his samples, then set out to gain control of all twenty thousand acres of Teel's Marsh.   It took several years to overcome competition and achieve complete success. Meanwhile, Smith established a partnership with his brother Julius, and a relationship through which his competitor, Coleman, became the sole East Coast agent for Smith Brothers. He and Coleman grew closer as time passed. On November 25,1874, he signed an agreement to borrow $10,750 "in gold coin" from the merchant, to buy up Teel's Marsh lands remaining outside of his hands. Later, the two became friends and shared in various enterprises, although without ever becoming formal partners. It was not surprising that the restlessly ambitious Smith wrote an associate soon after learning of Coleman's bankruptcy, "I will not attempt to disguise to you that I want the Coleman property."   For $580,000 in funds mostly borrowed from New York bankers he soon had it. He became the owner of Coleman's mines in the Death Valley region, his Calico property, and his processing mill in Alameda.[7]

Smith moved swiftly to exploit his new mine in the Calicos, holding in reserve for later development his acquisitions in the Death Valley area. Laborers erected board and batten bunkhouses, a dining hall, a store, a seldom-used reading room, a cabin for storekeeper William Washington "Wash" Cahill and his family, one for the mine foreman and his family, and a grand hilltop house near the head of Mule Canyon for Smith and other dignitaries to occupy when they visited the site. Christened "Borate" and never really large enough to be considered a town, the new camp became a center of activity. The site was an unlikely one. Fierce winds made it necessary to anchor the Smith house by means of cables from its four corners to bolts in bedrock. Oppressive summer heat and biting winter cold encouraged some of the miners always to live in the relative shelter of caves. The only families initially present were those of Cahill and of the foreman. As late as 1900, when the presence of a few more cabins reflected the arrival of a number of miners' families, Borate was chiefly a stag camp. At that, it was little more than an extension of Calico, and a very small company town.

Life was hard at Borate. Two shifts of men worked ten hours a day each, seven days a week, save for three and a half hours off on Sunday afternoons.   Miners at first received $3.50 a day, later after a wage reduction, $3.00, foremen, $7.00. The four hours daily when the mines were idle allowed smoke and dust to settle. The only holidays were St. Patrick's Day, July 4, Thanksgiving, and Christmas. Men who had lost their jobs with the closure of Calico silver mines constituted a large part of the work force. Chinese hands prepared food, for consumption in the company mess hall. Room and board initially was a dollar a day, then cost seventy-five cents after wages were cut.   Shopping in the company store was mandatory. Mine superintendent J. W. S. Perry was permitted to retain any profit remaining from the operation of the mess hall after costs had been subtracted from board receipts. Until Borate obtained its own post office, in 1900, Fannie Mulcahy twice weekly delivered mail by horseback from Calico. Homely as she was, the dollar apiece a month that the men paid was more than worth it for the chance to see a young woman—even though they seldom received any mail. The wife of Calico's Dr. Albert Romeo Rhea regularly drove her buggy to Borate to sell fresh fruits and vegetables. Hugh Stevens on Sunday afternoons often arrived in his three-seat spring wagon to take off-shift miners to Calico, for relaxation in a saloon.

Despite rough conditions, labor relations at Borate were placid. Like Calico, Borate was a nonunion camp. There were only two work stoppages, both brief.   Their dates have long since been forgotten, although it seems likely that both occurred close to the turn of the century. Neither was long enough or serious enough to dignify with the label, "strike." It is worth emphasizing, however, that singly and together they illustrate how economic issues can sometimes originate in cultural concerns. They also show how the latter—especially if they impinge on the domain of life that many of us regard as private—can become incendiary.

Surviving accounts of the first stoppage diverge in some details. "Wash" Cahill said that it began after Smith in Oakland bowed to Bay area sabbatarians who said that it was un-Christian to require Sunday work. He ordered that it cease, unaware that the nearest church was seventy-five miles away, in San Bernardino. Angry at the loss of a day's pay, the men walked out. Lucy Lane years later recalled that after a "volunteer engineer and fireman . . .[got] steam up," they commandeered a train at Borate and headed for the saloons of Daggett. She and Cahill differed as to destination saloons.   They agreed on several points, however.   The miners got "gloriously drunk" in Daggett. Within days the company restored Sunday work, conceding, as Cahill put it that "The men could work every damn day of the week if they wanted." The men returned to their jobs peacefully, although some of them needed another two or three days to sober up.

The second labor controversy grew out of foreman Fred Corkill's attempts to impose his own strict living standards on Borate's residents after his arrival in 1899. The men stoically endured threats of dismissal if they were found smoking cigarettes or with a sack of Bull Durham tobacco in their pockets. When beer was prohibited, they turned to bay rum. An order to pick up paper littering Borate and to economize by burning candles down to a designated length were too much to bear, however. The morning after receiving the directive, a crowd of muttering miners replied to the morning whistle by walking to Corkill's house, rather than beginning their shift. Corkill left his breakfast table to find out what was troubling them. After listening to a spokesman, he calmly replied that he would immediately pay off any dissatisfied workers and replace them, then reentered his house. Shortly, his wife appeared on the porch with a shotgun, while he wrote out pay checks. By the end of the day, the dissidents had been taken by train to Daggett. The incident might seem amusing to modern readers, but it is a stark reminder of the imbalance between capital and labor that obtained in the late nineteenth century.[8]

The borates on Smith's claims in Mule Canyon had originated through sedimentation on an ancient lake floor. Later, uplifting, folding, and faulting had shaped them into subsurface, discontinuous beds interstratified in lake sediments and occurring along a belt four to five miles long. There were two outcroppings. The main deposits lay in two workable seams about fifty feet apart. These were generally a few inches to twelve feet thick and concentrated along a linear distance of about two miles. Miners occasionally encountered large pockets of ore, some the size of houses. They called such pockets "kidneys." A crew of forty-five men sank an initial shaft at High Point, where the ore was richest, at an angle of forty-five degrees to the surface. The character of the deposits allowed use of typical subsurface mining techniques. Laborers sank vertical or high-angle shafts, ran drifts along seams or crosscuts at right angles to them, and excavated stopes. The stratified rock containing the borate beds was much more elastic and unstable than bedrock at the nearby Calico silver mines, requiring timbering. The overburden at some points compressed twelve-inch overhead crosspieces, or caps, to two inches' thickness in a year.

The complement of miners at Borate grew in a year to 120. Company workers in the district numbered 200 by 1898 and at last more than 600 in 1905 and 1906. At first, miners separated high grade ore from waste rock underground, by hand. They manually loaded fist-sized chunks of it into fifty-gallon whisky barrels, hoisted the barrels to the surface, and tipped the ore into chutes for loading into wagons. These carried it to Daggett, whence it traveled by rail to Alameda for refining in the plant that Smith had bought from Coleman along with his mines. After refining, the finished product entered the marketplace.

In 1890 Borate yielded about 23 tons of ore a day, or 700 tons monthly. Since San Bernardino County's entire refined borax product that year was about 980 tons, Calico's ores could not have yielded more than around 82 tons of refined borax a month. Perhaps 70 tons would be a more reasonable conjecture, given the existence of other smaller mines in the county in 1890. A year later, with a crew of 120 and Borate's mine in full operation, ore extraction reached about 70 tons a day, or perhaps 2,100 tons a month. At the turn of the century, it was over 100 tons, and at its peak in 1905 and 1906 it neared 130 tons, or 3,900 tons a month. In 1898 Smith's men sank a second shaft. By 1904 they were four hundred to five hundred feet down. Ultimately, working from two shafts and two drifts, they reached six hundred feet. By then, they employed standard mechanical lifts, hoists, and cages, powered by two, fifty-horsepower gasoline engines.[9]

Initially Borate's ores went to Daggett via a single wagon drawn by a ten-mule team driven by teamster Bob Gribben, who had briefly abandoned teaming to run one of Calico's saloons. As output grew, the company introduced a two wagon and twenty-mule team rig like those that had been designed in 1884 to move borax from Coleman's Harmony works, near Death Valley, to Mojave and Daggett. Jeff Riggs was the first teamster, Henry Chapman his swamper. Later, Charley White took over, with swampers Frank Tilton and Ed Pitcher, "who, after serving their apprenticeship each became 20 mule teamsters." Their "great wagons of the desert," "the largest . . . ever made," whose beds were four feet by sixteen feet by six feet deep, rolled on steel-tired five-foot front wheels and seven-foot rear wheels, and weighted 7,800 pounds empty. Teams straining out 120 feet ahead of them, rigs carried 45,000 pounds of ore, completing the circuit between Daggett and Borate in about two days and making twenty round trips a month. The first day of a trip they traveled five and a half miles from Daggett and made dry camp at a place called Mule Camp. The second day they climbed the steep trail into Borate, loaded, and returned to Daggett. On the following day they set out again, to repeat the circuit. In 1893 the company contracted with Seymour Alf and his eighteen-mule outfit, and then a second independent freighter with the same equipment, to move growing shipments of ore. The huge wagons and great teams represented a delicate equilibrium. The teams, twice the size of those previously employed, were as large as a single man could manage. Because they could pull two wagons and a water tender (if needed) with a single crew of two, they cut in-transit labor costs of desert freighting by half.

Nevertheless, Smith was not satisfied. Eager to cut transport costs still more, in 1896 he surprised local inhabitants by importing a huge, steam-powered tractor, such as those used in lumber camps, to speed shipments. Manufactured by the Daniel Best Company of San Leandro, the behemoth cost $4,500 and required a crew of three. Locals promptly named the gigantic machine "Old Dinah." Dinah drew two specially constructed

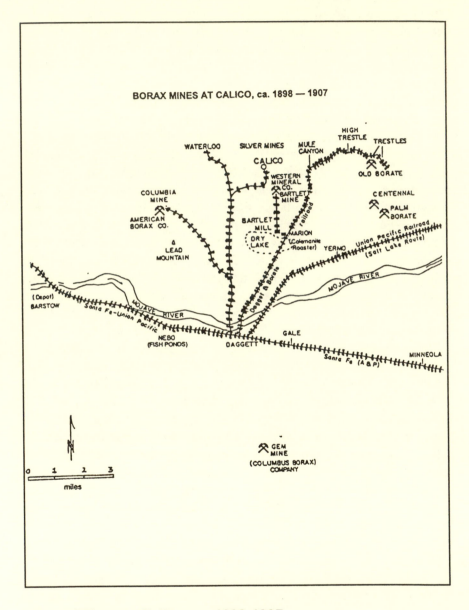

Borax Mines at Calico, ca. 1898-1907

Twenty-mule Team and Wagons Descending Mule Canyon. *Photo courtesy Mojave River Valley Museum.*

"Old Dinah" with Ore Wagons in Mule Canyon. Note decorative women. *Photo courtesy Mojave River Valley Museum.*

Locomotive No. 2, the "Francis," on Borate & Daggett R. R., 1907 [1906]. *Photo courtesy Mojave River Valley Museum.*

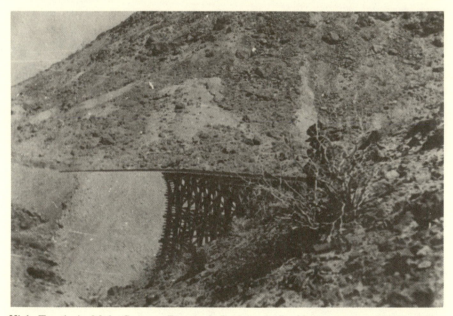

High Trestle in Mule Canyon, Borate & Daggett R. R. *Photo courtesy Mojave River Valley Museum.*

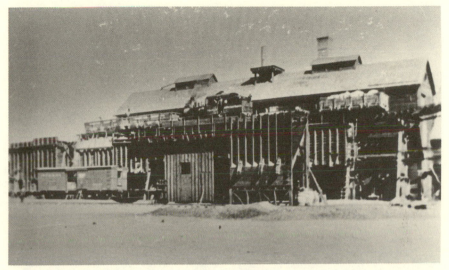

Marion Reduction Works, Pacific Coast Borax Company. *Photo courtesy Mojave River Valley Museum.*

Crew of Miners at Borate. *Photo courtesy Mojave River Valley Museum.*

Perspective of Borate. Note Borax Smith's house on hilltop. *Photo courtesy Mojave River Valley Museum.*

Mining Crew walking to work at Borate. *Photo courtesy Mojave River Valley Museum.*

14 GRANT AVE. SAN FRANCISCO. CAL

Francis Marion "Borax" Smith in his Fifties. *Photo courtesy Mojave River Valley Museum.*

wagons at three and a half miles an hour. On her first day of operation, Dinah "swung down the road past the store fronts and saloons [in Daggett] where a hostile crowd . . . loyal to the mule teams had gathered to watch," "expecting the new method of transportation" to fail. In the short run, Dinah doubled the output of the mule teams, completing a circuit in twelve hours, and Smith abandoned their use. But the tractor, when empty and traveling uphill, often reared up on its hind wheels. Worse, it dug itself into mud and soft sand and needed constant maintenance.   And it had a voracious appetite, consuming 2,500 pounds of coal per round trip. It was retired after a year.

Mule teams returned until 1898, when a railroad was completed from Daggett to Borate. The Borate & Daggett Rail Road was considered an engineering marvel. The line snaked its way steeply through, and along slopes above, Mule Canyon, crossing a spindly 500-foot trestle that coursed 100 feet above the canyon bottom, and then traversing two lower spans, before reaching its destination. With grades as steep as 8 percent, regular locomotives could not be used. The B & D R R employed instead two, geared Heisler locomotives, the "Francis" and the "Marion." These moved narrow gauge cars between Borate and a new refinery called "Marion," at the east end of Calico Dry Lake. A standard gauge 0-4-0 Porter locomotive, using a third rail, puffed between Marion and Daggett.[10]

As Calico borax mining peaked, in 1905 and 1906, other firms competed with Smith's. Employment in local mines, reduction plants, and refineries ranged "from 400 to 1600," depending on production and the season. The American Borax Company, founded in 1900, operated the Columbia Mine, near Lead Mountain about seven miles northwest of Daggett. Incorporated in 1901, it built a rail connection to the Calico & Daggett Rail Road, leasing from the latter track rights, and a locomotive to transport ore to its refinery in Daggett. The Western Mineral Company, 1896-1907, mined low grade ores where Odessa and Occidental Canyons met. It used mules to haul two ore cars and a flatcar one and a half miles between its mill at the foot of the mountains and its mine. Gravity brought the train back down, the mules and teamster riding the flatcar. In 1906 the Borax Properties Ltd. Company built a gravity railroad in Sunrise Canyon to open a mine on the east side of the Calico Mountains. The mine operated for no more than ten days. Smith had been anticipating the exhaustion of his Calico ores since 1903. Completion of the Tonopah & Tidewater Railroad now enabled him to shift operations from Calico to the rich Lila C. Mine near Death Valley. After yielding some 330,000 tons of ore and refined borax worth $20 million, Calico's mines closed in 1907.   Smith's workers took up the rails, disassembled buildings, and moved everything to the new location, or, in the case of Smith's house, to Ludlow.[11]

Borax was known in the ancient Mediterranean world. Imported via caravan from Asia, it became continuously available in Europe in the thirteenth century. Scarcity and resulting costliness confined its use chiefly to workers in precious metals, who employed it as a flux to cleanse oxides from surfaces and to reduce melting temperatures to aid welding and soldering. In 1750, it commanded £750 a ton in London. European sources were first found in the 1770s, in mineral springs in a desolate Italian valley. It was not until 1807 that Sir Humphrey Davy identified boron as one of the chemical elements. By then, several boracic fluxes had been developed for assaying metallic ores. Meanwhile, the Italian finds, by increasing availability, stirred a search for new uses. European output of borates reached seventy-five tons in 1828 and two thousand tons in 1860, while the London price fell to £100 per ton. By the 1830s the pharmaceutical uses of boric acid were well known. Within a generation followed discoveries of uses in enameling iron, making glass heat resistant, and cleansing. By century's end ingenuity had found new ways to employ borates: to preserve meats, harden plaster, aid in firing ceramics and making glass, assist in cement production, and facilitate manufacture of metals and rubber products.

Concurrently significant progress occurred in advancing knowledge of boron, which occurs naturally only in compounds with sodium, calcium, and magnesium, and never as a free element. The most important borax ore before the Calico mines opened was a fibrous material formed as heavily mineralized waters in desert marshes evaporated, inducing crystallization. The white crystals often clustered in spheres, from three to four to as many as eight to ten inches in diameter. Miners, because of the appearance of these borates, called them "cottonball." Cottonball in 1849 received the mineral name *ulexite*, for the German chemist Georg Ulex who first described its properties when he examined some specimens from Chile. Chemically, it is sodium calcium pentaborate octahydrate ($NaCaB_6O_9$. $8H_2O$).

Dr. J. A. Veatch first found ulexite in the United States, at some springs in Tehama and Lake Counties in California, in 1856. Extraction began in 1864 in California and Nevada, after commercially workable discoveries in some alkiline desert marshes. Happily, the material was amenable to crude, inexpensive processing. Laborers raked it into windrows at the marshes' edges, shoveled it into wagons, and transported it to refining sites. Because recurring seasonal evaporation continued to form cottonball, it was possible to repeat the collection process. As a result, operators called their work "farming." The refining technology was also primitive. It involved little more than 3,500-gallon wooden vats partly filled with water, some rubber tubes, settling tanks or ponds, and wood fires. Laborers dumped the cottonball into the vats, with sodium carbonate. The injection of steam warmed the water sufficiently to place the borates in solution. The calcium reacted with sodium carbonate, precipitating as calcium carbonate. The liquor was let cool to below seventy-seven degrees Fahrenheit, and borax crystallized on strings or wires, or in settling ponds. Repeating the process finally yielded 99.5 percent pure borax (sodium tetraborate decahydrate/$Na_2B_4O_7.10H_2O$). Since no crystallization took place when the fluid could not cool to less than 77 degrees, no processing occurred at desert sites during the heat of the summer.

The Calico mineral was different. Known as *colemanite*, which had been discovered by employees of William Coleman working near Death Valley in 1882, it is, chemically, calcium hexaborate pentahydrate ($Ca_2B_6O_{11}.5H_2O$), and it is much less soluable than ulexite. Exploitation had to await perfection of a practicable refining method. This turned out to be grinding the ore to the fineness of flour, then adding it to water. Heating and agitation, after the introduction of sodium carbonate, precipitated out calcium carbonate, and waste material settled. Boric acid, and borax in solution, remained. Cooling the liquor after it was drawn off allowed the borax to crystallize, on wire rods. The plant that was completed at Marion in 1898 introduced improvements. Two mechanical rabble (sweeping or stirring) arms moved the ore forward. A reverberating furnace with two hearths heated a roaster to 1,200 degrees Fahrenheit to roast (calcine) the ore. Calcining drove off the water in the ore and shattered (decrepitated) the borates into a fine powder. The process of screening followed, separating waste matter from the fines, or powered borates. The borates were then sent to Alameda for refining. Final purification, granulation, and bulk sacking for industrial use and packaging for home uses occurred at the Alameda refinery or at a new refinery that Smith had built in Bayonne, New Jersey, in 1898.[12]

Learning to process colemanite was only one of the problems that challenged Calico borate exploitation. Despite rapidly multiplying uses, prices crashed as western production shot up. They fell from 50 cents a pound in 1864, twenty-five cents in 1872 when it reached 1,000 short tons. In 1884, with 3,500 tons coming to market, they collapsed to less than ten cents.[13]

Against this background, Smith's activities and his mining of Calico borates were pivotal in charting the course of the industry. His first need, of course, was for capital. We have already seen that funds were needed to gain control of Teel's Marsh claims. They were also needed to provide for crude on-site processing there, although final refining took place at Coleman's Alameda mill. To these small initial requirements were later added $625,000 for purchase of Coleman's various interests and more to develop Borate:

> As to the size of the investment at Borate, we can only guess [wrote the archivist of United States Borax & Chemical]. There were three [two] completely equipped shafts of a possible total value of $90,000.00. Mining equipment in those days consisted only of rails, cars, picks, shovels, and hand drilling tools, blox shop equipment, etc., maybe $50,000.00 worth. The little camp . . . was nothing to brag about and could have been replaced for $30,000.00. The RR to Daggett may have cost $100,000.00 with loading bins and other facilities adding a possible $25,000.00 more. The calcining plant at Marion . . . may well in those days have cost $80,000.00. Give and take a few bucks and adding a couple 20 Mule Teams at $10,000 each we have $395,000.00 mas o' menos, as we say along the border.

Land for and construction in 1898 or a new, second refinery close to Eastern markets, at Bayonne, New Jersey, each cost another $100,000. Development costs for failed soap products before "Boraxo" was finally perfected, and miscellaneous costs, probably pushed capital needs through the period of activity at Calico to between $1.25 and $1.5 million.[14]

Frank Smith initially secured capital by forming a partnership with his brother Julius, who had prospered in farm implements in Chicago. The next step was the creation of a relationship with Coleman, both as the sole eastern sales representative of Smith Brothers, and as a source of credit himself as well as of access to New York bankers. Smith continued to take advantage of a widening web of personal contacts as well as of the contacts of his business associates. Repeatedly, he turned to borrowing to finance his expanding position in the industry. To a liberal use of credit he added dexterity in putting the receipts of his businesses to work. Of course, sales receipts could prove a further source of capital, but only if prices stabilized. Nevertheless, by 1880 Smith was strong enough to purchase, on his own, the bankrupt Pacific Borax Company and its works on Columbus Marsh, in effect using the credit of others by (probably) assuming its $45,000 debt to Coleman.

Four years later Frank ended his partnership with Julius, probably on unfriendly terms. Turning to develop his own properties on Columbus Marsh, he sold his interest in Smith Brothers to Julius. The deal required the latter to pay in borax at the prevailing market price. An unforeseen and ruinous price decline saddled him with a growing burden, from which he escaped only by selling the company back to Frank at a bargain figure. Having retained the right to use the name of Smith Brothers, Julius subsequently began to purchase refined borax and reentered the retail market. Frank bought Julius' right to the Smith Brothers name in 1893 for $6,000, and the latter afterward focused on operating a vineyard.

The challenge of market instability led Borax Smith in 1886 to initiate the second prong of his business strategy. This was to seek control of output and prices by dominating the industry. In striving for this objective, he repeatedly recurred to the use of credit, and to leveraging his own investment to govern ever larger entities. On March 29, he formed the Pacific Borax, Salt and Soda Company, with an authorized capital of $500,000 to be raised through the sale of 100,000 shares of stock at $5. Of this total, $38,000 had been subscribed. Smith, with 5,000 shares, was the largest stockholder. On April 20, the directors elected him president. They chose Joseph Wakeman Mather, who had been a commission agent for the California borax industry for its entire history and whose 1,000 shares were the second largest holding in the firm, vice president. Two weeks later, the directors agreed to purchase Smith's 16,000 acres of borax lands near Columbus, Nevada, together with his company store and its merchandise. He was to received "for and in consideration of the above mentioned property . . . One Hundred Thousand Shares of the Capital Stock of this Company. . . ." The Mather connection proved crucial, for Mather placed at least $70,000 of his own funds at Smith's disposal as well as opening to him new channels to New York bankers.[15]

The following year, on October 5,1887, with the continued cooperation of Coleman, Smith led in forming the "San Francisco Borax Board." This body brought together all five United States producers in a cartel—Smith's Pacific works and Teel's Marsh Borax Company, Coleman's Harmony Borax and Meridian Borax Companies, H. L. Coye's Nevada Salt & Borax Company, Emil C. Calm's Columbus Borax Company, and John W. Searles's San Bernardino Borax Company. Voting strength in the cartel, which priced refined borax at seven and a half cents a pound, was based on the relative size of participants' operations, as were sales allocations. Smith received twenty-eight votes and a 1,400-ton annual allotment; Coleman, twenty-four votes and 1,200 tons; Coye, nine votes and 450 tons; Calm, five votes and 250 tons; and Searles, ten votes and 500 tons. All sales were to be made through the Board, and members bound themselves to $5,000 fines for each breach of the arrangement. The agreement was terminable on November 1,1890, "or at any time thereafter by six months' notice given to the Board in writing . . . ." The Board met monthly for about eighteen months, with immediate profits for Smith and the others. At the end of November, 1887, Pacific Borax, Salt and Soda declared a dividend of $1 a share on 5,000 shares of $100 each of restructured capital. Dividends continued at this level every month, giving Smith and his nominees an income of about $58,000 a year. Prices remained at seven and a half cents until a business depression struck in 1893.[16]

On January 29, 1888, Smith made his next major move, resigning from the board and the presidency of Pacific. He was apparently still the largest and most influential stockholder. Three weeks later, on February 18, he communicated a proposal to the company's directors. He offered to purchase Pacific's entire inventory of about 650 tons of borax for six and a half cents a pound, for resale on the open market at seven and a half cents. The deal was concluded at the end of the month. Of the $83,675.66 due from Smith for the borax, he had to pay only $5,000 out of pocket. He paid $42,633.20 by canceling a company debt to him in that amount, another $7,467.00 by taking borax in payment of a note from Mather, and the final $28,557.46 with a note of his own. Almost monthly for eighteen months after, the company accepted an offer from him to buy borax at six and a half cents for resale on the market at seven and a half cents. This arrangement assured him a nice profit on monthly production of 145 tons. With the acquisition of Coleman's mines and refinery, on March 12, 1890, with funds obtained from New York banks through Mather's assistance, Smith was the premier figure in the industry. He recognized that quick exploitation of the rich, easily accessible colemanite in the Calico claims was the key to a consolidation of his position as the foremost producer. It also promised economies that would make marsh mining of ulexite obsolete. For the next decade and a half the property gave him advantages that no rival could successfully challenge. Not least among these was time to plan how best to exploit the former Coleman properties around Death Valley, when the Calico ores were exhausted.

In October, Francis Marion Smith launched the Pacific Coast Borax Company, of which he was principal stockholder and president. Although the prospectus was lost in the San Francisco fire, evidently he included in its capitalization 15,000 shares of voting stock with a par value of $100 per share. He exchanged with it the assets of Pacific Borax Salt and Soda, his Teel's Marsh properties, and the Coleman claims—described as being "of vast extent, and of assured excellence" of ore—for 5,000 shares of its stock. He aimed, according to a surviving letter, to sell but 1,000 of its remaining 10,000 shares. His position was enviable, "fortified," as one account put it, "with dividends, sales commissions and cash from the sale of borax [to consumers] bought from his own company with . . . 6 percent notes which he issued . . . ."[17]

A half dozen years later, when depression severely curtailed trade, he traveled to England in search of new markets. While on shipboard, he chanced to meet an acquaintance who had contacts with an English chemical firm seeking sources of borax: Redwood and Sons. A day of negotiations brought an agreement on August 16, 1896, to form the Pacific Borax and Redwoods Chemical Works, Limited. Incorporated in Britain, it commenced business with an initial capital of £310,000 of common (at a par of £10), £200,000 of 6 percent preferred (also at £10 par), and first mortgage bonds of up to £100,000 as might be needed. Smith again leveraged control, conveying to the larger new entity the assets of Pacific Coast Borax in return for a principal interest in it. He completed his quest for hegemony in 1899 with the organization of a multinational firm, Borax, Consolidated, Limited. B. C. L. united the Pacific Borax and Redwoods Chemical Works Limited, the remaining important British firms, and the two leading French firms. Among the firms absorbed were the English Borax Company, Limited and the Societé Lyonnaise, both of which owned mines in Asia Minor. Through these it controlled important mines in the U. S. Turkey, Chile, Bolivia, and Peru, as well as marketing arrangements with the German and Austrian borax industries. Smith held the dominant interest in B. C. L., although he confined his activities to this country and let European directors attend to affairs elsewhere. Voting stock, of which he held a highly-leveraged majority, was only 25 percent of the authorized capital of £2.4 million. All of the preferred stock and the authorized debentures were offered for sale; none of the common was. The formation of B. C. L. gave the industry very much the form in which it continues today.[18]

Smith's corporate career after the turn of the century needs only brief mention here. Foreseeably, it continued on a mercurial course. In 1899 he conceived a scheme to create a new, pyramided American holding company. It was to assume his interests in B. C. L., including the Pacific Coast Borax portion of the former's assets, as a means of providing new collateral against which he could borrow. He aimed to control the new entity, which would in turn control B. C. L. The plan would let him dominate B. C. L. while reducing his investment in it. The directors rejected the idea promptly, but he tried to revive it in 1901 and 1902. He also began in 1899 quietly to lend surplus B. C. L. funds to himself on call. Considerable sums were involved: $600,000 in 1904 alone. These resources he used to build up a real estate and transit empire. He purchased every electric trolley line in Contra Costa and Alameda Counties, a ferry line connecting Oakland and San Francisco, and large tracts of land for development. In 1912 with two associates he formed the United Properties Corporation, to hold their combined assets. Overextended and unable to cover short-term notes, it passed into trusteeship in May 1913. Smith's $20 million fortune soon evaporated. He sold shares in B. C. L. to pay creditors, and he severed his connection with Pacific Coast Borax. Between 1921 and 1925 he began to develop new colemanite holdings in Clark County, Nevada. His fortunes seemed to be improving when he died in August 1931.[19]

The third prong of Smith's business strategy was consistently to advocate a protective tariff for borax products. Mather performed a useful role in this effort, relocating to New York after the death of a son and persuading Smith to open an office there on January 1,1889, at 148 Wall Street. During congressional consideration of tariff revision in 1883, 1888, 1890, 1893, and 1897, Smith and his associates weighed in with letters and publications directed to the House Committee on Ways and Means, emphasizing the importance of protective duties. Their efforts were particularly strenuous in 1888 and 1893, when Democratic majorities threatened to place borax on the free list. The 1893 appeal of U. S. producers entitled *Borax Products of the Pacific Coast: Facts and Figures Regarding Borax* collected and reprinted communications sent to the Committee over the past dozen or so years. The piece stressed the importance of borax, its many uses—more than fifty applications were cited—and the potentially devastating effect of foreign competition if protection were to be removed. There is abundant evidence that these efforts paid off. Democratic efforts to place borax on the free list failed in 1888 and again in 1893 and 1894. The 1883 tariff imposed *ad valorem* duties of 76.08 percent, 119.47 percent, and 42.31 percent respectively on boric acid, crude, and refined borax. The McKinley tariff of 1890 raised the rate on boric acid to 95.12 percent, retaining those on crude and refined borax unchanged. When the Senate finished gutting the 1893 House bill with the addition of 634 protectionist amendments, the new rate on boric acid stood at 57.06 percent, those for crude and refined borax at 79.64 and 57.06 percent respectively. The Dingley tariff of 1897 hewed to the same protectionist policy, taxing imports of boric acid and refined borax at 129.6 and 71.48 percent. Able to produce crude borax at lower cost than any competitor, Smith was content to have it placed on the free list.[20]

The fourth element of Smith's strategy was a constant effort to reduce costs. His use of twenty-mule rigs applied animal power on an industrial scale to the transportation problem. As borax prices fell, he turned next to "Old Dinah," and finally to a railroad at Borate. The construction of a mill at Marion greatly improved the efficiency of processing, among other things making the manual sorting of ore from waste unnecessary. The Bayonne, New Jersey, plant offered additional economies. Smith introduced the use of reinforced concrete in building the plant, and replaced the customary steam engine driving a main shaft with separate electric motors to furnish motive power for milling ores. Augurs propelled raw material to the upper floor of the plant, allowing reliance on gravity in various steps of processing. The new mill sheltered a separate production line for making packaged borax for home use and had a yearly capacity of 12,000 tons, that at Alameda about 8,000. The former employed two hundred, the latter a force reduced by more than half, to eighty. After the century's turn, the Alameda facility ceased operations. Meanwhile, the shipment of partially processed, walnut-sized chunks of high-grade ore running 40 percent or more in borax content from Marion to Los Angeles, then to England, for refining allowed still further savings.[21]

The final component of Smith's strategy was to increase demand for borax. The inability of industrial consumers to take up more than about half of output presented a serious problem. Industrial research toward developing new products for household use, and advertising to encourage consumption, were key lines of action. Promotional efforts began in the 1870s, largely at the instigation of Julius Smith. Even in the context of the wildly exaggerated advertising of the late nineteenth century, his claims stand out. Borax would, among other things, improve the cleaning action of laundry and washing water; counter the toxic substances in soap that caused lung fever and kidney trouble; make skin beautiful; and used as a shampoo would likely delay "premature decay of the mental faculties."[22]

Such assertions were only the beginning. A born promoter, J. W. Mather pushed the campaign to new heights, quadrupling sales during his first year of work in New York. A year later his son, Stephen Tyng Mather, then a reporter for the *New York Sun* and later the first Director of the National Park Service, came on as a part-time adviser and soon as a full-time employee. It was he who conceived of using the story of the twenty mule teams to romanticize and publicize borax. Smith at first opposed the idea, commenting, "No, I cannot say I like the idea of the 'mule team' brand of borax. My name and that of the company should be in the foreground." He yielded after John Randolph Spears, a fellow reporter at the *Sun* whom young Mather induced to take on the task, published *Illustrated Sketches of Death Valley and Other Borax Deserts of the Pacific Coast* (1892). First serialized in the *Sun* and then reprinted as a book, it captured the imagination of the reading public and quickly became a small classic, its promotional origins forgotten.   Soon an illustration of the teams and wagons, with the "Twenty Mule Team Borax" label, became the company trade mark.

The recognized uses of borax were impressive enough.   Where truth ended, hyperbole took over, adding claims that borax ". . . purifies water . . . arrests diphtheria . . . relieves hoarseness . . . insect bites . . . cures cracked tongue . . . heals ulcers and boils . . . relieves acidity of the stomach . . . prevents proud [badly swollen] flesh wounds . . . cures skin diseases and eruptions . . . relieves burns, bruises, and sprains, [and] allays inflammation and prickly heat." It also treated "sore mouth and gum boils," killed insects, prevented the pox, and staved off cholera.   Mather circumvented Smith's initial opposition to paid advertising by writing letters purportedly from housewives for publication in household magazines, extolling borax. He planted syndicated stories about borax in newspapers. He added coupons to borax boxes promising a dollar to any consumer who published a letter to an editor about borax. In 1903 a twenty-mule team and rig were sent to the St. Louis World's Fair for daily exhibition. Before long, merchants who purchased twenty-five or more cases of one-pound household packages of "Twenty Mule Team Borax" or other company products could arrange for a traveling twenty-mule team and rig to visit their establishments. Smith became an advertising convert, and was spending $300,000 a year on promotion by 1906. He had after several years of experimentation developed a new product for home use, a perfumed cleansing formula named "Boraxo," and an unscented companion, "Grime Off," to join "Twenty Mule Team Borax." A new definition even entered the vernacular—"borax"—meaning cheap goods acquired through redemption of coupons obtained from "Boraxo" and "Twenty Mule Team Borax" boxes.[23]

When we take the measure of these efforts, some striking things become clear. Smith's enterprise, based on mining a relatively obscure mineral, was arrestingly successful. As early as 1893 the federal report on mining activity set national output of refined borax for 1891 at 6,690 tons. Of this, 5,000 tons came from the Pacific Coast Borax Company's works, chiefly at Borate. The remainder was divided between four other vastly smaller firms, The San Bernardino Borax Company at Searles Lake and three other sites (900 tons); the Nevada Salt & Borax Company (550 tons); the Columbus Borax Company (240 tons); and Consolidated Borax (360 tons). Smith within a year of opening his Mule Canyon mine accounted for 70 percent of the nation's output. The prospectus for Borax Consolidated, Limited securities, claiming too much while probably expressing B. C. L.'s long-term aims, said that its holdings were "believed to comprise all the important mines and sources of production of raw material from which nearly the whole supply of the world has hitherto been obtained." In 1905 an official federal report referred to the Borate mine as "the most productive of all the mines . . . ." A 1910 report observed, "It is this locality which has furnished, for a period of more than a dozen years, practically all of the borax obtained in the United States." So it was. Between 1902 and 1906, total sales in the United States of the Pacific Coast Borax Company rose from 10,500 to 12,500 short tons. Of this sum, 25 percent was to meat packers, and sales of products to household users had grown to equal these. Virtually all of the production was from the Calico mine. By 1905, Borate's annual refined output averaged 25,000 tons. This figure was roughly half the world total, which included 10,000 tons from Chile; 9,000 from Turkey; 5,000 from Peru; and 2,700 from Italy.[24]

The importance of borax mining at Calico surpassed even the fascination of its story. It was there that borax extraction first moved away from the marshes and entered "an entirely new era . . . . Thenceforward the industry was transformed into a proposition akin to that of quartz mining and allowing an abandonment of the necessarily rough methods of the marsh system of production." Too, the Calico borates, and those mined subsequently at other sites, "opened up a new and permanent supply [in the form of colemanite] and in quantity sufficient for whatever demand might be made upon it."[25] Besides, the local mines participated from the outset in the wider life of an industrializing national economy. It would be difficult to justify any use at all of the term "frontier" in referring to them, for they operated no less than Calico's silver mines in an area governed by national, state, and local authorities and a formally organized mining district. Finally, Borate and other area operations were indistinguishable in appearance from company camps all over the West—thrown-together, all-male, evanescent. As other extractive western ventures, they had to look to the populous East for both capital and markets. Like local silver mines, they depended on an imported, mature deep-rock mining technology with its reliance on mechanical hoists, railroad transportation, power-driven mills.

Smith repeatedly employed technological advances to cut costs and maximize profits, whether turning to industrial-scale mule-drawn wagon rigs, "Old Dinah," railroads, gasoline engines, electric motors, powered augurs, reinforced concrete in structures, or new and improved refining processes.   Faced with output that outran the demand of industrial consumers, he turned to research to develop new household products, and to advertising to create a market for them in order to expand sales. Ceaseless promotion established widely-recognized brand names, and a pattern of advertising that continued well into the twentieth century through such varied outlets as publications, development of Death Valley as a tourist destination, promotions including the sale of models of twenty-mule teams, and radio and television programs.[26]

At another level, control of the colemanite deposits in Mule Canyon bought time and generated the means with which Frank Smith could consolidate his hegemony over the industry. The chain of mergers that he engineered after adding the Coleman properties to his own took full advantage that his Calico mine was the most productive in the world, and that its easy access to railroads provided an inexpensive means of transporting its large and valuable yield. It also placed him at the center of structural changes that set the corporation at the center of the nation's metamorphosing economy. His repeated use of leverage to finance his growing corporate holdings positioned him at the forefront of entrepreneurs of his time. A desire to control production and thus stabilize prices led him to form, finally, a multinational combine that dominated global borax output and marketing. When Calico's borates were exhausted, Smith's foresight and resources enabled him to be ready to shift operations to Death Valley.

Smith's and other Calico mines and his industry were, it is true, comparatively small. To use an imperfect but suggestive analogy they recall—when considered with other lines of extraction of industrial minerals—Walter Prescott Webb's comparison of cattle ranching in the West with cattle raising in the East. Millions of farmers in the East conducted a huge business on a small scale, running a few head apiece on their farms. Ranchers in the West, on the other hand, raised fewer head of livestock in the aggregate. But they conducted their comparatively small business on a magnificent scale. So it was with the Borate mines at Calico, and with Smith. If this perspective seems too fanciful, then Smith can surely be placed in the company of a rising and visionary new class of businessmen who were creating structures that could impose control, order, and stability on production and markets in an emerging industrial economy.   His enterprises lay in an underdeveloped and dependent region. But they were in no sense colonial, subject to external control. There was no mistaking who dominated them, nor his shrewdness in identifying and exploiting an opportunity niche. There was also no doubt where the profits accumulated. In these regards Smith ranked with such other figures as John D.

Rockefeller, Andrew Carnegie, and J. P. Morgan, and his Borate operations compared with pivotal stages in their advance to preeminence.

NOTES

1. An earlier version of this chapter was published in *Montana: The Journal of Western History*. I am indebted to the editor and the anonymous referees for suggestions that greatly strengthened it.
   Quotations, Edwin Corle, "Calico Days," *Yale Review,* 30 (Spring, 1941), 551; also Corle, *Desert Country* (New York: Duell, Sloan & Pearce, 1941), 297-98. Warren Dean Starr, "History of the Settlement and Development of Calico, California, to 1900" (unpublished M. A. thesis, Washington State University, 1963), 82-84, repeated and embellished Corle's tale, drawing also on Harold Weight, "Gray Ghost of Calico," *Westways*, 41 (March, 1949), 14-15; and Lucille Coke, *Calico* (Barstow, 1941), 21. For context see Robert Wiebe, *The Search for Order, 1877-1920* (New York: Hill and Wang, 1967), which provocatively treats contemporary economic and social change, for issues of economic dependency and colonialism, Richard White, *"It's Your Misfortune,"* esp. 27-60. For a brief summary of the development of the borax industry, Anonymous [Ruth C. Woodman and Ann Rosener], *The Story of the Pacific Coast Borax Co. Division of Borax Consolidated, Limited* (N.P.: Borax Consolidated, Limited, 1951).

2. Quotations, copy of *Calico Print* in possession of Harold O. Weight, *Twenty Mule Team Days in Death Valley* (Twenty-Nine Palms: The Calico Press, 1955), 37; Lane, *Memories*, 44. See also Norman J. Travis and E. J. Cocks, *The Tincal Trail: A History of Borax* (London: Harrap Limited, 1984), 60-64; and, for Stevens' claims, "Index to Mines, San Bernardino County," II-III, *passim*. Among Stevens' locations were the Sam Houston No. 3, the Carbon Mine, the Carbonite, the Veteran, the Maio, the Lone Star, and others.

3. Lane, *Memories*, 44; Weight, *Twenty Mule Days*, 37. Although Starr got the story wrong about the discovery of Stevens' claims, he did report the sale price correctly.

4. For Stevens, Lane, *Memories*, 8; for Coleman's first efforts, *Mining and Scientific Press*, 46 (June 9, 30, 1883) 389, 437.

5. Richard P. Rothwell, Ed., "Borax," *The Mineral Industry, Its Statistics, Technology, and Trade*, 2, 6, 7, 8 (New York: The Scientific Publishing Company, 1894, 1898, 1899, 1900), respectively 74-76, 61-63, 90-96, 64-67; provides the most detailed statement of production in San Bernardino County, and Calico, 1882-1897. For a broader view, compare with figures in Joseph Struthers, Ed., "Borax," *The Mineral Industry, Its Statistics, Technology, and Trade*, 9, 10 (New York: The Scientific Publishing Company, 1901, 1902), respectively 57-59, 65-689. Also Fletcher H. Hamilton, "Monthly Report of Chapter XVIII of the State Mineralogist," *Mining in California* (Sacramento: State of California, 1922), 689; Charles G. Yale and Hoyt S. Gale, "Borax," *Mineral Deposits of the United States, Calendar Year 1912: Part II, Nonmetals*, 2 (Washington: Government Printing Office, 1913), 893-96; and George Herbert Hildebrand, *Borax Pioneer: Francis Marion Smith* (San Diego: Howell North Books, 1982), 31, 49.

6. Travis and Cocks, *Tincal*, 48, depending on James B. Scherer, *The Lion of the Vigilantes: William T. Coleman and the Life of Old San Francisco* (Indianapolis: The Bobbs-Merrill Company, 1939), 309-10, set Coleman's liabilities at $2 million, against assets of $4.5 million. Hildebrand, *Smith*, 32-33, 41, erroneously pegged liabilities at $20

million. In either event, Coleman lacked cash to meet current obligations.

7. Quotations, Travis and Cocks, *Tincal*, 42, which treats the Smith-Coleman relationship 42-48; Weight, *Twenty Mule Days*, 38. For background, Hildebrand, *Smith*; Scherer, *Coleman*.

8. Lane, *Memories*, 42, 43-44; William Washington Cahill, "NOTES ON OPERATIONS AT OLD BORATE AS RECALLED *BY . . . WHO WENT TO WORK THERE IN 1892*" (unpublished, undated manuscript in possession of the writer), 1; Ruth C. Woodman, "History of the Pacific Coast Borax Company" (unpublished manuscript, 1969), in Ruth C. Woodman Papers, Department of Special Collections, University of Oregon Library, Chapter VII, 34-41; Travis and Cocks, *Tincal*, 64.

9. Henry G. Hanks, *Fourth Annual Report of the State Mineralogist* (Sacramento: State of California, 1884), 225; Marius R. Campbell, *Borax Deposits of Death Valley and the Mohave Desert* (Washington: Government Printing Office, 1902), 12-14; Richard P. Rothwell, ed., "Borax," *The Mineral Industry. Its Statistics, Technology, and Trade*, 6 (New York: The Scientific Publishing Company, 1898), 62-63; Charles G. Yale, "Borax," *Mineral Resources of the United States . . . 1889 and 1890* (Washington: Government Printing Office, 1892), 494-506; Charles R. Keyes, "Borax Deposits in the United States," *Transactions of the American Institute of Mining Engineers*, 40 (1910), 674-710; Hildebrand, *Smith*, 62-64; Travis and Cocks, *Tincal*, 60-64. For a capsule history of activity at Borate, William E. Verplanck, "History of Borax Production in the United States," *California Journal of Mines and Geology*, 52 (July, 1956), 276-83.

10. William Washington Cahill to Ruth C. Woodman, January 12, 1949; and Cahill, "HALF A CENTURY WITH THE PACIFIC COAST BORAX COMPANY AND SUBSIDIARY COMPANIES" (unpublished manuscript, undated); Woodman, "History of Pacific Coast Borax," all in Woodman Papers.

11. Wagon and workforce quotations, Anonymous, "Borax—Early and New Methods of Production," *The Scientific American*, 82 (May 26,1906), 326; Old Dinah quotation, Lane, *Memories*, 42-43; Smith's house, Cahill to Woodman, January 12,1949, in Woodman Papers. Also John A. Delameter, "My 40 Years Pulling Freight," *Touring Topics*, 22 (August, 1930), 24-29; Weight, *Twenty Mules*, 25-44; Alan Baltazar, *Calico and the Calico Mining District, 1881-1907* (Barstow: Alan Baltazar, 1995), 42-46; Gordon Chapell, "By Rail to the Rim of Death Valley: Construction of the Death Valley Railroad," *Journal of the West*, 31 (January, 1992), 10-20; Travis and Cocks, *Tincal*, 61, 119-20; Hildebrand, *Smith*, 62-64. Verplanck, "History," 282-83, reported on the brevity of activity in Sunrise Canyon. He also noted that the Columbus Borax Company worked a mine about four and a half miles south of Daggett, outside of the Calico district proper. For production, Richard P. Rothwell, ed., "Borax," *The Mineral Industry,* 8: 57-59; Yale, "Borax," *Mineral Resources . . . 1908*, 2 (Washington: Government Printing Office, 1909), 603-5.

12. Detailed discussion of technology, Yale, "Borax," *Mineral Resources . . . 1904*, 1,017-1,028; Anonymous, "Borax," *Scientific American*, 326; Bernard E. Loe, "An Analysis of the Economic Significance of Mojave Desert-Death Valley Borax Mining Operations, 1872-1963" (unpublished master's thesis, University of Redlands, 1963), 4ff; Baltazar, *Calico*, 39-42. For the plant at Marion, also Verplanck, "History," 281.

13. United States Geological Survey, *Mineral Resources of the United States, 1915*, Part II, "Nonmetals," (Washington: Government Printing Office, 1917), 1,017.

14. H[arrison]. P[reston]. Gower, archivist, personal letter to the writer, March 28,1958. Born in 1890, Gower went to work for Pacific Coast Borax in 1909. His *50 Years in Death Valley—Memoirs of a Borax Man* (N. P., 1969) contains few references to Borate, although it does detail the fate of "Old Dinah." For the Bayonne facility see Hildebrand, *Smith*, 46-47 and *passim*.

15. "Articles of Incorporation March 29,1886"; quotation, minutes of directors of April 30,1886; summaries of minutes of all stockholders' and directors' minutes to October 28,1890, in "Material on PACIFIC BORAX SALT AND SODA COMPANY" (unpublished notes, undated), in Woodman Papers.

16. "COPY OF AGREEMENT. 15 OCTOBER, 1887" (unpublished manuscript), quoted, 4; in Woodman Papers. Also, for prices, Rothwell, "Borax," *Mining Industry*, 2(1894), 74-76.

17. "COPY OF MEMORANDUM" (unpublished, included in minute book of Pacific Borax, Salt and Soda Company), quoted, 1; in Woodman Papers.

18. "MEMORANDUM relating to the formation of BORAX CONSOLIDATED LTD., prepared by Mr. [R. C.] Baker, undated" (unpublished manuscript, undated), Woodman Papers.

19. Hildebrand, *Smith*, 32-33, 41, 44-45, 52-57, 152-257, and *passim* differs in some details from the account presented above, which follows Travis and Cocks, *Tincal*, xi-xii, 42-48, 62, 67, 73-75, quoted, 49. Woodman, "History of the Pacific Coast Borax Company," Chapters VI, VII, and VIII, although a rough and scarcely legible pencil draft is useful; also Loe, "Borax," 19.

20. Borax Producers of the Pacific Coast, *Borax Products of the Pacific Coast: Facts and Figures Regarding Borax* (N. P., September 1,1893); United States 53 Congress, 2 Sess., *Senate Report* No. 559, "Comparison of the Customs Law of 1894 and the Customs Law of 1890" (Washington: Government Printing Office, 1894); 53 Congress, 1 Session, *Senate Report* No. 707, "Bulletin No. 61, Part I. Committee on Finance, United States Senate. The Customs Law of 1894" (Washington: Government Printing Office, 1894), 1; *Senate Report* No. 708, "Bulletin No. 62, Part II. Committee on Finance, United States Senate. Statistical Tables" (Washington: Government Printing Office, 1894), 3, 108; and United States 55 Congress, 1 Sess., *House of Representatives Report* No. 1, "Proposed Revision of the Tariff" (Washington: Government Printing Office, 1897), *Senate Document* No. 188, "Comparison of the Tariff Act of August 28,1894 . . . [with that of 1897]" (Washington: Government Printing Office, 1897), 2, 4; Woodman, "History of Pacific Coast Borax," Chapter VI, 31, VIII, 10, 53-54.

21. Yale, "Borax," *Mineral Resources . . . 1906*, 1,059, . . . *1908*, II, 603-5, . . . *1912*, II, 839-46; Hildebrand, *Smith*, 46-47. Cahill, "Notes," 1, recalled that only ores richer than 45 percent went to England for refining. Travis and Cocks, *Tincal*, 1-8, working from company records, set the figure at 40 percent.

22. Travis and Cocks, *Tincal*, 45.

23. Borax Producers, *Borax Products*, 1; Smith quoted, Travis and Cocks, *Tincal*, 66, see also 44-45, 66-68, 114-15; Hildebrand, *Smith*, 268-74 and *passim*; John Randolph Spears, *Illustrated Sketches of Death Valley and Other Borax Deserts of the Pacific Coast* (Chicago: Rand McNally & Company, 1892).

24. Changes in accounting methods make it difficult to chart both borax production and its value, from the 1880s through the closure of the Borate mine. Through 1902, reports tracked the quantity and value of refined borax. After 1902, they recorded the quantity of *ore* produced, and its value at the pithead reckoned in terms of 1 percent of a $120 per ton value for refined product for each percent of borax in the ore. The result was an apparent

vast increase in output and decrease in price. Recurring to the former accounting practice and arbitrarily assigning a 15-17 percent average, borax content to ore yields an imputed output after 1902 that is comparable to that for preceding years. Such an adjustment is also consistent with a refined borax price that held at seven and a half cents for five years after the formation of B. C. L. See Yale, "Borax," *Mineral Resources . . . 1905*, 1,092-96, quoted 1,093; Keyes, "Borax Deposits," *Transactions*, quoted 694; Travis and Cocks, *Tincal*, 1-8, 114-16, quoted 85, cited 25,000 tons of refined product, an output comparable with that of previous years. Also Anonymous, "Borax," *Scientific American*, 326, for consumption by meat packers; David T. Day, "Borax," *Mineral Resources of the United States, Calendar Year 1891* (Washington: Government Printing Office, 1893), 587-88. Yale, "Borax," *Mineral Resources . . . 1906,* 1,059-62, and "Borax," *Mineral Resources . . . 1907*, 631-35, gave the 1906 price as seven and a half cents. The opening in 1907 of the Lila C. Mine, with its lower cost of production, prompted a drop to four and a half cents.

25. Quotes, Anonymous, "Borax," *Scientific American*, 326.

26. See for examples, Anonymous [Woodman and Rosener], *Pacific Coast Borax Company*; United States Borax and Chemical Corporation, *The Story of Borax* (Glendale: United States Borax and Chemical Corporation, 1979).

Chapter 4

CALICO FINDS ITS VOICE:
THE *CALICO PRINT*

. . . we simply say, 'This is a newspaper.'
Calico Print, July 8,1882

Much of what we know of Calico is a direct result of the arrival there, in June, 1882, of John G. "Johnny" Overshiner. Overshiner was a native of Ohio, born in Galena in 1851. Before his birth, his father had succumbed to "gold fever" and rushed west to seek wealth in the placer mines of the Sierra Nevada foothills. Johnny left the Buckeye State as an infant. While yet less than a year old, he accompanied his mother on the arduous, storm-tossed voyage around Cape Horn as part of the human tide flooding into California. He grew up in the Golden State. When it was time to take up a trade, he became an itinerant printer. He came to Calico from San Diego, filled with ambitions and hopes, intending to publish and edit a newspaper.[1] The first issue appeared soon after his arrival, although there is no way now of establishing exactly when he reached the camp. Imaginatively named the *Calico Print*, his feisty weekly left an indelible mark on the town for which it was named. Its story is inseparable from that of Calico.

Overshiner, his paper, and the community needs that it served are best understood when viewed in light of some of the most striking distinctions of the nineteenth-century United States. Calico was an "instant community"—a place to which settlers rushed in hopes of quick fortune after hearing news of rich silver discoveries there. It was a local variation of a theme perfected and played out again and again as Americans poured across the Appalachians and streamed westward across the continent to seek fresh beginnings or fortunes in farming, town planting, minerals, transportation, commerce, finance, real estate, and whatever other opportunities beckoned. It epitomized places of its sort, and the hopes of those who hastened to it. They were a restless, transient population, and they could be a fickle one. When compared with Europeans and their more settled habits, these Americans seemed astonishingly rootless and mobile. They might decamp as quickly as they had arrived upon receiving a report of some new prospect beckoning elsewhere. If they remained, lifting reality to the level of their ambitions was often a formidable challenge. Where newly arrived settlers saw prosperous farms, bustling enterprises, and thriving communities, travelers and passersby might see only a tiny collection of tents, shacks, and clutter strung along a single dusty or muddy, rutted road, or widely scattered and primitive farmsteads. That is where boosterism came in.

The most visible, prominent booster was often the local newspaper. How else for newly arrived merchants to publicize their wares, for town planters to attract settlers, and for a paper itself to prosper except through promotion? How else for editors and publishers, who were often one and the same person, to survive in such communities than by advertising into existence as real towns the unpopulated reality in which they typically began their labor? The symbiosis between ambition, town, and paper was a natural one. Each fed on the others. Ray Allen Billington captured the matter perfectly in he wrote in *America's Frontier Heritage*, "Westerners could appreciate the story of the stranger who asked how one small town could support four newspapers and was told that it took four newspapers to support such a town."[2]

The booster spirit of the American press waxed with the advance of settlement farther and farther west. As it did so, it displayed "an ever greater willingness to take risks," and encountered a corresponding increase in the possibility of making mistakes. Recurring cycles of speculative boom and bust left maps cluttered with the names of places that had never really materialized, or that had withered after greatly foreshortened lives. Their papers died with them. As Daniel Boorstin observed, "Hovering about every ghost town was the spirit of one or more ghost papers, relics of advertising that had failed. Again and again, ambitious migratory newspapermen aimed not at the known needs of some existing community but at the needs of some future community for which they desperately hoped." In doing so they advanced claims whose extravagance could outrun truth, mingling prevarication with ambition. Meanwhile, multiplying nascent western communities promised more to printers than advertising and circulation revenue. There were town and county ordinances to print, tax and other government legal documents to publish, and all manner of forms and notices about proving out homesteads, filing mining claims, and sundry real estate transactions to circulate. An enterprising editor could also expect, if all went well, to generate a steady income from designation as the official local government printer, and from job printing.

There was more. Boosterism could wear many faces. A newspaper could meet several needs of transient new arrivals. It could acquaint them with local conditions, giving them information useful for the conduct of their affairs and providing them with a feeling of neighborhood. It could nourish a sense of shared communal identity and pride. It could affirm that civilized standards persisted, even at the far edges of the settled regions. It could call for needed local improvements and reforms. Performance of these functions depended on the editor. It was easier for him to take them on for several reasons. Small, portable, hand-operated presses (some cost as little as $150) allowed convenient access to new communities at minimum costs. Despite the growth of railroads, of telegraph lines, and more recently of telephone systems, the day of mass communication still lay in the future. Life was intensely local. One key to success in publishing newspapers was to anchor them firmly in their immediate communities. This fact allowed journalism to be both local and personal, as it often was.[3] At one end of the spectrum of this small town journalism lie thousands of evanescent papers remembered—if at all—like their editors, in name only. At the other stood William Allen White and his *Emporia* (Kansas) *Gazette*, which became its premier icons and most enduring symbols. Overshiner, Calico, and the *Print* stood squarely within this tradition, and somewhere between its poles.[4]

The first issue of the *Print* appeared on July 12, 1882. Its publication granted the town, almost at the moment of its beginning, a journalistic voice through which to inform its people and the wider world of its affairs. The new journal announced its birth lustily. The most important feature of its first issue was the obligatory statement of purpose expected of every contemporary editor on such an occasion:

CALICO PRINT

According to the oft-repeated anecdote a painter, who was just mounting the first round in the ladder of artistic fame, attempted to depict on a canvas an equine quadruped, and apprehensive that there might be a doubt in the minds of some as to the species of animal it was meant to represent, wrote below in bold letters the inscription, 'This is a horse.' Apprehensive that the casual observer of this sheet [the *Print*] might think that it was a common piece of fabric sold at fourteen yards for a dollar, which blushing brides are so loath to clothe themselves with after being [a]rrayed in orange blossoms, silk, and satin, during a brief and blissful honeymoon—we simply say, 'This is a newspaper.' It is not an organ. It will not be used to grind out some favorite tune or hobby regardless of the effect it may have on our readers. It will be used to publish the most reliable information concerning the rich mining districts of San Bernardino county, also concerning the agricultural, vinicultural [sic], grazing, mercantile, and varied business interests, as well as important and valuable news from all parts of Southern California. We shall endeavor to furnish our subscribers with a paper that they will be proud of, and take pleasure in sending to distant friends. All of the business interests of this place [Calico] will be benefitted by a live newspaper, and we will take pleasure in making it such if we continue to receive the encouragement and support we have already received since we arrived in this camp. Fifty-two yards of this CALICO PRINT will be sold to each subscriber annually for four dollars, and we can assure you that all who make such an investment will find it a profitable one. We will assure you its colors will never fade so long as we receive a generous supply of the 'color' [silver] that is being daily taken in abundance from some of the many rich mines of the district.

Overshiner could hardly have written a more appropriate maiden column. He said everything that was needed to launch his paper. He promised unimpeachable integrity, reliable information about all lines of business, and a publication of which Calico would be proud. He pledged a nonpartisan commitment to the camp's interests and needs. He offered good value, fifty-two issues for about eight cents each. He held out the prospect of profits for his readers.

The contents of the first number of the *Print* confirmed the sound business sense and grasp of the requirements of small town journalism that ran through Overshiner's first column. It was a paper of four pages, each twenty-four by thirty-six inches in size. Its masthead displayed its name in bold letters, with a reproduction of the Great Seal of the State of California inserted between the two words. The remainder of the first page was given over mostly to poetry, serialized fiction, and advertisements filling the two left-hand columns. A box at the upper left beneath the masthead carried vital information. Subscriptions were $4.00 for the year, $2.00 for six months, or $1.25 for three months, payable "in advance." Readers also learned, "Advertisements inserted at reasonable rates." Items printed on page 1 set a pattern followed subsequently. Among them were "When Stars are in Quiet Skies" (a poem), "Behind the Scenes" (a short story), "London Sights," "Scenes at a Bull Fight," and "A Nice Place to Live in" (all travel fillers). The second page held state and local news, and two columns of commercial notices at the right side. Local news followed on the next. The fourth and last printed the by-laws of the recently formed Calico Mining District in the left hand column and a half. Its remainder consisted of ads.

Advertisements took up about a third of the initial issue. With the passage of time, they came to occupy even more space, occasionally more than half. The paper held to this format throughout its existence. Its enterprising editor had already recruited advertisers in San Francisco, Los Angeles, San Bernardino and neighboring Colton, Grapevine, and Calico. By July 27, he had arranged for the entry of the *Print* as second class matter at the Calico post office, to facilitate inexpensive circulation through the mails.[5]

The editor-publisher of the *Print* had arrived in Calico well-prepared to enter business. He brought with him a prized Washington hand press and several cases of type. He had lined up advertisers. A full staff of helpers was on hand as he occupied space in a hastily constructed building on Calico Street.   I. Benjamin of San Bernardino and Oscar Morris of East Calico were typesetters. E. Clarke and William Burtnett did the press work. Partner E. E. Vincent was the printer. Mid-1882 seemed an auspicious moment to introduce a paper in Calico, which was experiencing its first burst of growth.

Publishing a newspaper at the edges of civilization was not easy. The first page of the first issue of the *Print* carried a date of Saturday, July 8. The inside pages were dated Wednesday, July 12, when the paper actually came out. Overshiner's type had reached Calico "pied" in its shipping cases. It took several days to sort and set it. Despite the delay, the first edition made at least one positive impression. The *Los Angeles Times*, in a rare charitable mood, commented favorably. It praised the "first issue of this long looked-for paper" as being "newsy and sparkling with wit . . . ." Even better, it praised Calico's newcomer for containing "much valuable mining information and the laws of the camp." After describing the *Print* as a six-column paper and identifying its publishers, the *Times* concluded that it bore "marks of careful editing."[6]

Usually. During slow news seasons, the paper could sink to abyssal depths. On one such occasion it devoted much of its front page to a piece intended to be humorous, describing how a woman kisses "a tobacco chewer." The reader discovered that after "a preliminary shudder . . . she sets her teeth hard, holds her breath, and makes a little pigeon dip at the foul lips of the grinning beast . . . ." Immediately afterward, "pale with horror," she flies to the kitchen "where, if you follow her, you will find her disinfecting with soap and water." The writer continued that many women could successfully pretend that they like "the smell of a cigar, but even hypocracy [sic] is powerless to force from a woman the confession of a fondness for hanging like the bee on a flower to a tobacco worm's lips."

Even writing such as this held some redeeming qualities. It may have prompted some readers to laugh. It probably encouraged others to feel a bit of pride, since its author was one of Calico's women. It may even have helped sales of the paper.[7]

Ever alert to possibilities for increased business, the publishers of the *Print* three weeks after introducing it changed the day of publication "from Saturday to Thursday, in order to avoid the inconvenience of having the papers of outside subscribers remaining in the Post office several days before the departure of the mail."[8] In September Overshiner bought out Vincent and became sole owner and publisher. Although Calico's population continued to swell during the following months from the five hundred to eight hundred of the summer of 1882, he sensed a fresh opportunity as crews laying tracks for the new transcontinental railroad neared. Mining discoveries in the Ord Mountains to the southwest, and completion of the railroad, promised to make Daggett the regional commercial and transportation hub. Prudently retaining the name of the *Print,* Overshiner removed his office to Daggett six months after beginning publication. By 1885, his younger brother, Harry, had become the typesetter. A nephew, Lloyd, worked as "printer's devil," helping with all manner of tasks in the shop and occasionally taking on an assignment as a cub reporter. The men all lived with Overshiner's sister, Mrs. William O. Swinnerton, who completed what had become very much a family business. The *Print* remained in Daggett until February, 1886. Then, with Daggett "making no progress and Calico being on the boom . . . the *Print* office" relocated back to Calico. Before it halted publication, the paper changed the day of publication at least one time more, to Sundays.[9]

Regardless of place of publication, the *Print* vigorously performed its several roles. It could always expect to stir readers' interest by responding to real or imagined slights of Calico. When the *Tombstone* (Arizona) *Epitaph* claimed that its name "would lead one to believe that it is a 'Dolly Varden' sheet," that is, effeminate, and poked fun at its editor's name, there was a ready reply: "It overshines a graveyard inscription anyhow."[10] Attacks from other quarters brought equally prompt rejoinders. Overshiner got into a journalistic brawl with the *Los Angeles Times* over its advocacy of Sunday closure laws. He condemned the *Times* for a disregard of individual liberty and of separation of church and state—positions that could hardly have been unpopular with the miners among his readers. When the *Times* termed Calico a den of iniquity, he asserted. "Although we have no church building nor preacher to officiate in it, yet there is not a more orderly mining camp in the United States." After the *Times* acerbically reported that "There is no ground for a Calico boom," and headlined that Calico was "A Good Place for Poor Folks to Stay Away From," he returned to the hustings. Business, the *Print* claimed, was "exceedingly dull" in the City of the Angels. As for poverty in Calico, the town was not at fault for it. Such poverty as existed was not the result of bad business conditions. Rather, it was the wages of individuals' "improvidence, speculation, and the overindulgence of sensual pleasures." [11]

Whatever the appeal of spirited defenses of Calico to readers, these were among the least important of the methods a country editor could employ to promote his town. Overshiner used a full complement of tactics. He made certain that his paper enjoyed a regional, rather than a merely local, appeal and usefulness. Its principal "range of circulation" came to include "all the mining camps of the Mojave desert, as Providence, Ivanpah, Mescal, Alvord, Oro Grande, Grapevine, Death Valley, Calico, Daggett, Barstow, etc., and the principal towns of the county." It steadfastly retained its focus on "mining interests and local news." More revealing was the fact that it was, by 1886, regularly "mailed to 50 post offices inside and 40 outside of the State." Overshiner made certain that Calico's prospects and news received the widest possible exposure. Among regular recipients of his paper was the mining industry's foremost periodical, the *Mining and Scientific Press*. The *Press* for its weekly report of local activity depended on the *Print*, whose regular mailings to it in turn assured national visibility for the camp and its mines. [12]

As far as circumstances allowed, and sometimes farther, the *Print* claimed that Calico faced a promising future. A January, 1884, story quoted in the *Mining and Scientific Press* enthusiastically reported, "There is [sic] at least 300 men . . . in the Calico mining district, busily engaged in getting out ore and developing the various properties . . . ." More important, the Oro Grande mill had "turned out $400,000 of bullion from the [Silver] King mine within the past ten months," that at Hawley's Station had "shipped $300,000 of bullion to San Francisco during 1883, and the Oriental mill . . . about $200,000 . . . in the same length of time." [13] Seven months later the *Press* again quoted the *Print*, noting, "The various mines of the Calico district are constantly improving . . . . East Calico especially is developing some very fine properties, and somewhere in Oriental canyon we expect a town to spring up that will vie with Calico. Near the Bismarck mine about 250 men are working." [14] There is good reason to suspect that Overshiner was, in April, 1886, the "gentleman from Calico" who gave the *San Bernardino Weekly Times* "a glowing account of that mining camp . . . ." This gentleman, the *Times* said, had reported several important new strikes, including a "well-defined ledge beneath the iron crust and at a depth far below anything ever found . . . in the Calico district. If true fissures exist in the region," the *Times* added, "as seems to be the case from recent developments, Calico will be a second Comstock."[15] That December the hand of Calico's editor-publicist may again have been at work when the *Los Angeles Times* announced, "'King Calico' is having a baby boom in his baby kingdom."[16]

The *Print* remained faithful to its formally nonpartisan political stance throughout its existence. Political independence carried advantages, not least that of not offending partisan readers whose business it needed. Independence also contributed important freedoms in separating advocacy of civic improvement from political entanglements. The paper could and did promote the interests of Calico's townspeople—or, at least the whites. Predictably, it displayed the anti-Chinese prejudice that tainted life across the West. A story entitled "Chinese Filth in an Anti-Chinese Camp," decrying the accumulation of human excrement in Calico's Chinese quarter, was characteristic.[17] The journal successfully campaigned for the formation of a town sanitary commission, in the winter of 1884 and 1885. The need for improved sanitation persisted, however. The following May found Overshiner commenting that the town was "positively filthy in some quarters, and the accumulation of nastiness is on the increase."[18]

The editor was also politically active himself. He ran unsuccessfully for constable in 1882. He assisted in bringing a public school to Calico. He was elected a school trustee in 1885.[19] His civic interests extended to promoting the formation of a local literary society. He could be counted on to promote varied cultural causes, such as "A grand Musical and Literary Entertainment . . . given by the Ladies of Calico . . . for the benefit of the [Town] Hall."[20] Likewise, he championed the cause of fair pay for miners. In 1882, when local mine operators attempted to reduce miners' daily wages, he spoke out strongly for the maintenance of a $4 daily pay scale: "Considering the nature of the work . . . [miners] have to perform and the danger and hardship they have to encounter, $4 a day is little enough. This is a $4 camp."[21] Falling silver prices forced him to recant in July 1885, when mine owners cut wages to $3. "Miners," he wrote, "must accept the inevitable." Given that silver prices were "on the decline," there were "few mines that can afford to pay $4 a day . . . ." Even this retreat could be regarded as an attempt to promote Calico. If miners accepted lower rates, the mines could stay open, miners could retain their jobs, and the town could prosper.[22]

Taking the largest possible view, the *Print's* politics placed it in the country's vigorous traditions of egalitarianism, hostility toward monopolies and excessive concentration of economic power, and suspicion of politicians and government. Writing of the 1882 campaign, Overshiner wearily—or was it warily?—noted that voters would learn from candidates of the astonishing "corruption and unworthiness" of candidates on the one side and the wonderful "purity, faultlessness, and superior ability" of those on the other. For him it would be enough to elect "officers that are upright, opposed to monopolies, and who will not forget the rights of the poor while seeking the favors of the rich." Unless politicians kept their promises better than formerly, voters would lose what little confidence they still retained in them.[23] His most ample surviving political statement appeared two years later when he wrote:

WHAT OUR VOTERS WANT

The voters of Calico are more interested in who shall fill the office than in any particular party issue presented to the people at this time by the different political bodies. It matters not whether a Democrat or a Republican is elected, the Sunday laws will prevail, Chinese will be employed, and corporations will form monopolies as far as they can under the law, we all know that. But we want representatives capable of understanding our needs who will keep unjust burdens from being imposed on us by corporate power, and who will see that taxation is made equal between all, that all may bear their equal share of the public burden as far as possible.[24]

Political nonpartisanship had its limits. These coincided with the interests of silver mining. It was no coincidence that the *Print* spoke favorably of the nominees of the 1882 California state Democratic convention at San Jose. It maintained that the residents of Calico "heartily endorsed" the Democratic ticket offering General George Stoneman for governor and John Daggett for lieutenant governor. Should Stoneman be elected, Overshiner injected in the news account, "he will make an able and efficient governor . . . ." Two years later the editor took pains to advertise the contributions of miners to the nation's prosperity. He remained a staunch defender of silver and conscientiously endorsed whichever nominees would promote it. On at least one occasion he launched a forthright attack on "The Unprincipled Banks." A two-column tirade alleged that they were trying to ruin the government, cause a financial panic, and destroy small business.[25]

Whatever it was and did as a promoter of Calico, the *Print* never lost the qualities of personal journalism with which it had begun. It was always a projection of its editor's persona and beliefs. The nature of the town and society that it served reinforced these characteristics. Given Calico's isolation and small size, word of local events spread quickly through conversations. What was news today could be very stale days later when the weekly paper came out. It was up to the editor to find ways to lend interest to accounts of events that might be well known by the time the paper appeared. His views, as a result, did much more than shape editorial columns: they insinuated themselves into news stories, personal notices, even advertisements.[26] The results were nearly always interesting and sometimes comic.

Consider, for example, how the *Print* dealt with this request from a reader. It reported that "one of the fortune hunters among these bonanza mountains of the Mojave desert [sic] approached and confidentially buttonholed us," asking that no items be published "concerning him which may have happened during the past two or three weeks . . . until he got sober." The story did not identify the person to whom it referred. It did not need to, since scarcely anyone in town could have avoided knowing who it was.[27]

Then there was the tactic of converting a lack of news into news. "Not even a fight to chronicle this week: verily ye reporter has a hard time finding news when there is none to be found." Or, "The camp is becoming duller and hotter every day," as spring gave way to the heat and slower pace of summer. Again, there were "just as many men at work as ever before, but the boys evince a disposition to keep their coin in their pockets." Given these conditions, it is easy to understand why the closure of the Calico school for the year "with appropriate [but undescribed] exercises" and the departure of the teacher via coach to Los Angeles was deemed worthy of notice.[28]

Events of much greater moment, if generally known, might receive comparably brief treatment while allowing Overshiner to perform as guardian of community morals. Witness, "John Doe was killed at the Pastime [a dance hall]. Good riddance."[29] He could enact the same part at much greater lengths where stories held greater potential for edifying or entertaining his readers. In one instance he put a comic twist on the readiness of some of his fellow citizens to resort to wild west gunslinging:

Last Monday two boys (old boys) got loaded with somebody's best, loaded their pistols, and then proceeded to unload them. The manner of their unloading was as unique as it was dangerous. Both lay on a bed together and utilized the door knob as a target. John fired three shots and as he failed to hit the door, Fred thot he could do better. But Fred had probably never handled many pistols, and was not aware that they sometimes kick. Taking the weapon in his hand with the aim of an accomplished shootest he fired and hit—the knob? no, his nose—when he pulled the trigger he neglected to hold the pistol tightly, and the consequence was the stock hit him in the smeller, and tumbled him out of bed.   Realizing that something had happened, the nature of which, however, he was not exactly sure about, he jumped up and accused John of attempting to murder him. Little boys should not fool with big pistols.[30]

Overshiner tolerated prostitution, which was a regular feature of mining towns. When patrons' complaints led to arrests of "two proprietors and sixteen of the 'frail but fair employees'" of one of Calico's dance halls, for robbery, he reported the affair good humoredly. In his account of the waiver of most of the complaints on petition of Calico's best citizens, he sympathized with their contention that a $30 fine was too severe a penalty for the women to bear. He agreed, too, that prostitution in the center of Calico was less an evil than it was as practiced in the residential districts of San Bernardino. Even here, it was possible to assert civic superiority of a sort. Robbery of blameless victims was a different matter, though, whether or not the loot was valuable. Of one theft he warned, "The man who took Barstow's egg-shaped pipe is known and he had better return it to this office. Various small things ar[e] missing in camp and the guilty parties had better return the property or leave at once."[31] He reserved his greatest outrage for offenses against Calico's leading, most respectable citizens. The classic expression of his anger at uncivilized conduct resides in an account of an incident that disrupted the May Day Ball and Ice Cream and Strawberry Festival of 1885. The ladies of Calico had arranged the event as a fund-raiser toward paying for the newly completed town hall. About 2:00 a.m. on May 2:

a most disgraceful and outrageous assault took place in front of the hall, the full particulars of which we are not prepared to give in this issue. From the confused accounts of the affair that have reached us we briefly give the following. James Patterson, superintendent of the Occidental and Garfield mines, who was present at the dance, was requested to step out of doors, as some one wished to see him. He proceeded to do so accompanied by two of his friends, James Marlow and W. E. Stoughton. Just as they reached the front door they were greeted with a volley of eggs, and Mr. Patterson was struck in the face with a rock or sand bag. Several volleys of eggs were thrown before the parties had time to draw their guns, and as soon as they did draw . . . the assailants fled, one of them, W. H. Foster, running through the hall, while Marlow pursued him firing several shots, none of which took   effect . . . .[32]

The assailants turned out to be employees of a rival mine. They were apprehended and punished. So was Marlow, for "shooting up" the town hall. In other mining camps, where pick handles or even bullets were preferred to eggs, such an encounter could easily have resulted in one or more fatalities. Recollections of this affair survived among former residents of Calico through the 1950s, one more indication of the impact on their memories of contention between John S. Doe and his rivals.[33]

In the end, events betrayed Overshiner's ambitions and cut off the brief life of his paper. The hopes for a boom with which 1886 ended went unfulfilled. Much worse, and decisive for the *Print*, fire roared through Calico on September 4,1887, destroying the town's heart. Overshiner got out one last issue, an extra printed on bedsheets because all of his newsprint had been consumed in flames.[34] Afterward he moved, with his press, to Needles. There he worked with F. H. Haber on *Our Bazoo*. This paper underwent a number of name changes, to *Booth's Bazoo*, then *The Needles Eye*. Later, the press traveled to Greenwater camp, near Tonopah, Nevada. It continued to migrate from one printer to another, unrecognized for what it was. Finally, in 1950, while it was on loan from San Bernardino's Inland Printing Company to Harry Oliver, publisher of *The Desert Rat Scrap Book*, its identity was rediscovered. That year Walter Knott, owner of Knott's Berry Farm in Buena Park and nephew of the same sheriff, John King, who had grubstaked the discoverers of the Silver King, purchased it. It remains in the print shop at Knott's Berry Farm to this day.[35] Overshiner himself wound up in Wilmington, California, where he died shortly after the turn of the century. Even though we cannot now gauge the *Print's* effectiveness as an agent of Calico's development, its profitability, or much of its history, it is Overshiner's monument.

It is also our most important source for Calico's story. All told, between July 8, 1882, and September 5, 1887, some 270 issues were printed. Presently, four are known to survive in the library of the Society of California Pioneers in San Francisco and another twenty in the Bancroft Library of the University of California, Berkeley. Several others extant as late as the 1950s have disappeared. These include one from the winter of 1882-1883 that Harold Weight owned when he wrote *Twenty Mule Team Days in Death Valley* (1955); the October 18,1884, issue that Yermo law enforcement officer Tom Williams possessed; the October 10,1886, edition formerly held by the Los Angeles County Museum; and the 1887 bedsheet edition once owned by desert pioneer and Daggett resident Dix Van Dyke. Quotations, many of them lengthy, from the *Print* appeared often in the *Mining and Scientific Press*, 1882-1887. Others were printed from time to time in other California newspapers, especially the *Los Angeles Times*, the *San Bernardino Weekly Times*, and the *San Francisco Chronicle*. Altogether, directly or indirectly, it is possible to get at perhaps thirty-five to forty issues. These offer an indispensable glimpse into the life of Calico. They are also a telling example of late nineteenth-century American booster journalism.   As such they are illustrative of the vital economic, informational, and cultural roles that newspapers played in community development.   While regretting that so many issues of the paper were lost, we can be grateful for those that survive.

NOTES

1. Scant information survives about Overshiner's life. That furnished in this chapter derives largely from Zoe Foard, personal letter to the author, November 21,1957. Ms. Foard was Overshiner's niece.

2. Ray Allen Billington, *America's Frontier Heritage* (New York: Holt, Rinehart & Winston, 1966), quoted 81. The standard reference for many years has been Frank Luther Mott, *American Journalism; A History of Newspapers in the United States Through 260 Years: 1690-1950,* revised edition (New York: The Macmillan Company, 1950).

3. Daniel Boorstin, *The Americans: The National Experience* (New York: Vintage Books, 1965), 124-134, quoted 127, is the beginning point for any serious discussion of boosterism and its place. Earl Pomeroy, *Pacific Slope: A History of California, Oregon, Washington, Idaho, Utah, and Nevada* (Seattle: University of Washington Press, 1965), especially 155-58, noted that Pacific Coast journalists tended to be more partisan than those in the interior. For urban development generally, Charles N. Glaab and A. Theodore Brown, *A History of Urban America* (New York: The Macmillan Company, 1967), 107-33, remains useful. For the isolated, local conditions of existence, Robert Wiebe, *The Search for Order, 1877-1920* (New York: Hill and Wang, 1967), 1-10, 110, remains powerfully suggestive.

4. Sally Foreman Griffith, *Home Town News: William Allen White & the Emporia Gazette* (New York: Oxford University Press, 1989) offers the most subtle, sophisticated, sustained discussion available. Also useful are Lewis Atherton, *Main Street on the Middle Border* (Bloomington: Indiana University Press, 1954); Michael Frisch, *Town into City* (Cambridge: Harvard University Press, 1972); Robert Dykstra, *The Cattle Towns: A Social History of the Kansas Cattle Trading Centers of Abilene, Ellsworth, Wichita, Dodge City and Caldwell, 1867-1885* (New York: Atheneum, 1970); and Don Harrison Doyle, *The Social Order of a Frontier Community: Jacksonville, Illinois, 1825-70* (Urbana: University of Illinois Press, 1978).

5. *Calico Print*, July 8, 27,1882,

6. *Calico Print*, July 27, 1882; *Los Angeles Times*, July 18,1882.

7. *Calico Print*, July 8,1882.

8. *Calico Print*, July 20,1882.

9. *Los Angeles Times*, December 4,1886. Lucy Lane, *Memories,* 1-2, recalled details about Overshiner and his family.

10. *Calico Print*, October 21,1882. Dolly Varden was a character in Charles Dickens' novel, *Barnaby Rudge*. Many western mines bore her name, which could also refer to a dress of sheer-figured muslin worn over a brightly colored petticoat.

11. *Calico Print*, July 20, 27,1882, February 22,1885.

12. *Los Angeles Times*, December 4,1886; *Mining and Scientific Press*, especially 46 (May 10,1883), 341-54 (May 21,1887), 336.

13. *Calico Print*, January 12,1884, quoted in *Mining and Scientific Press*, 48 (January 19,1884), 36.

14. *Calico Print*, July 16, 1884, quoted in *Mining and Scientific Press*, 49 (August 2,1884), 72.

15. *San Bernardino Weekly Times*, April 10,1886.

16. *Los Angeles Times*, December 1,1886.

17. *Calico Print*, July 8,1882.

18. *Calico Print*, May 10,1885.

19. *Calico Print*, May 31,1885.

20. *Calico Print*, March 1,1885.

21. *Calico Print*, July 8, 1882.

22. Lane, *Memories*, 2, quoting *Calico Print*, July 19,1885.

23. *Calico Print*, July 20,1882.

24. *Calico Print*, October 21,1884.

25. *Calico Print*, July 8,1882, June 21,1885.

26. Griffith, *Home Town News*, 1-9; and Fr. Walter J. Ong, *Orality and Literacy: The Technologizing of the Word* (New York: Methuen, 1982), are very suggestive in considering the characteristics of oral and literate cultures.

27. *Calico Print*, July 8,1882.

28. *Calico Print,* May 31,1885.

29. *Calico Print*, October 18,1884.

30. *Calico Print*, May 31,1885.

31. *Calico Print*, February 22, March 8,1885, and July 8,1882.

32. *Calico Print*, May 10,1885.

33. *Calico Print*, May 10,1885; author's interview with Lucy B. Lane, March 28, 1956.

34. *San Francisco Chronicle*, September 5, 11,1887; L. Burr Belden, personal letters to the author, November 2,1957, February 20,1961, January 18,1965. Belden, a writer of historical columns for the *San Bernardino Sun-Telegram*, saw a copy of the bedsheet edition, which was in the possession of desert pioneer Dix Van Dyke. For the disappearance of the Los Angeles County Museum issue of the *Print*, Dorothy E. Martin, personal letter to the author, April 20,1956.

35. Anonymous, "Old Printing Press Found," *Calico Print*, 7 (July, 1950), 6. Although carrying the name and continuing the volume numbers of the original *Print*, this publication was a monthly. Its editors-publishers were Larry and Lucille Coke. The place of publication was Daggett.

Chapter 5

Saturday Night in Calico: Life in a Mining Camp

What, Take that boy . . . into that wild mining camp . . . ? No! NO!
Mother of Herman F. Mellen, 1882

Visitors to Calico today can purchase a booklet on the back cover of which is a reproduction of a mural entitled "Saturday Night in Calico, 1881." The mural itself was painted about 1950. It covers a wall in a building about 150 miles from Calico, named the "Calico Saloon" and standing in a tourist park called "Ghost Town, California." The view is up Calico Street. Above the school house at the end of the street illuminated sheds, bunkhouses, headframes, and black plumes of coal smoke mark the entrances to eight or so mines on the dark slope of King Mountain. About a dozen commercial establishments flank either side of the unpaved, rutted roadway, which is filled with people. Prostitutes are visible standing in the windows of the second floor, and in the door of the closest building on the left, whose sign says, simply "ROOMS." Adjacent is Joe's Saloon, which advertises a "Dance Tonight." Abutting Joe's is a second saloon, and Lane's Mercantile Store stands beyond. A covered wagon obscures the front of the next building. At least one team, one pack animal, and one saddle horse are visible. The lettering on the false fronts of the remaining structures is more or less illegible.

So is the lettering on the buildings across the street until we read "Town Hall" on that immediately in front of us. People throng the streets, conversing, staggering out of saloons, carousing and falling to the ground with whisky bottles in hand. At least two couples are in evidence. One is well-dressed and strolling sedately amid the clamor. The other consists of a man who is attempting to escape from a woman clutching his coattail. There are two dogs in view. The first is hoisting a leg next to a post. The second is chasing a cat. The warm glow of coal oil lanterns within buildings shines through doors and windows, casting oblong rectangular patterns into the street. Street lanterns on posts add to the warmth of the scene.

The mural is suggestive. Unfortunately, it hints more at stereotypes and an imagined Calico than at reality. It is filled with anachronisms. There was no Town Hall in 1881. In fact, there was no town in 1881. Lane's General Mercantile came into existence only in the 1890s. Dance halls were a prominent feature of the scene when Calico was flourishing, although not one is in evidence in the mural. These are only a few of the errors that would stand out if our concern were with the accuracy of the painting. Our interest in this chapter lies elsewhere. Here we aim to get beyond suggestions and misconceptions and explore some of the chief features of life in Calico as its inhabitants experienced it.[1]

It would be a serious overstatement to claim that Calico was all business. It would be no less serious an understatement to propose that Calico did not know what its business was, or that its business powerfully shaped the flow, ebb, and character of life there. Calico originated and made its living as a mining camp. The lure of mineral wealth attracted its population. Mining provided incomes for the overwhelming share of its residents, both miners and those whose businesses served miners and mine operators. Something like 90 percent of all those employed in the vicinity were either miners, millers, or craftsmen on mine payrolls. Like mining towns generally, it attracted people from a wide range of geographical backgrounds. There was a prominent contingent from Pioche, Nevada. There were a few—at least a good-sized handful—who had been criss-crossing the West in a quest for mining fortunes since the California gold rush of 1849. There were Mexicans, Germans, Greeks, Frenchmen, Englishmen (including arrivals from the Isle of Man), Swedes, Chinese, Australians, highland Scots, numerous Irishmen, and veterans of the first rush to Alaska, at Juneau. The Odessa Silver Mine began the use of miners from Cornwall, England, the descendants of generations of tin miners. As many as half the employees of the Garfield Mine were Cornishmen. They were regarded locally as among "the best miners as a whole that the world could boast, having followed the trade, father and son, for centuries."[2]

The economics of silver mining governed the local economy. Calico's array of businesses waxed and waned with its population. Its population grew or shrank with the level of activity in local mines. Mining depended, in turn, on the national and international silver market and the monetary policies of governments as these bore on the demand for silver.

In July 1882, when perhaps five hundred souls had flocked to the site, most of Calico's buildings were still either tents or frame. Twenty-five frame houses joined as many tents as residences along the single street that the narrow bench running alongside Wall Street Canyon could contain. Miners and prospectors continued, too, to grub dugouts and caves in the walls of canyons in the vicinity. There were already three dozen or so businesses to meet local needs, including the *Calico Print*. Some occupied tents, others, wooden structures hastily cobbled together from whatever lumber could be obtained. Two attorneys, a notary public, a shoemaker, and seven saloons (several with barbers and all with gaming tables) offered their services. An assayer, a livery stable, a druggist, a post office, and the office of Dr. Rollin "Rollie" Austin Goodenough (whom locals called "Dr. Drunkenough") added to the list. There were several eating places, and a meat market provisioned with stock from Jack and Annie LeFurgey's ranch on the river at the site of the former Hawley's Station. Newcomers arrived daily, taking advantage of the "new, Light-running, Easy-riding Concord Coach" of the Calico Stage Line. Six public boarding houses and hotels already awaited them. The most notorious was the Hyena House, several hollows beneath a rocky ledge, protected from the elements and partitioned into rooms by flimsy walls fashioned from barrel staves. Proprietors Bill Harpold and Dick Hooper shamelessly promoted it to unsuspecting newcomers. The former greeted each incoming stage with a wheel barrow and the announcement that it was a conveyance providing transportation to their hostel. Their guests endured execrable accommodations and a breakfast of chili beans and whisky.[3]

Calico's rocky desert situation posed difficult problems. Before water wells were dug close to town, the precious fluid came either from the Mojave River or wells along its course and sold for as much as fifty cents a gallon. In July, 1882, "with two wells" completed, two "Bronchoes" made frequent deliveries to the camp, where water was sold for five cents a gallon. Even with this reduction, water remained expensive. Complaints about its cost continued. By 1885, the Silver King Mine had a well that flowed at 300,000 gallons a day and was said to provide an "inexhaustible" supply of water. The Calico Water Works Company's well, dug an eighth of a mile from that of the King, remedied the problems of a supply for domestic use and of expense. Teams drew water wagons from this well at the edge of the dry lake, near the Garfield Mill, to two redwood tanks on Tank Hill, which lay just south and a bit east of the camp. Gravity flow carried it through a system of pipes from the tanks to consumers in town. The new arrangement worked very well. The price of water fell to $1 a month for single consumers, $2 for a man and wife, and $3 or $4 for families, depending on size.[4]

Sanitation was in some ways a more intractable difficulty. As early as July 1882, the editor of the *Print* complained of the use of Wall Street Canyon and ravines behind the buildings lining Calico Street "for the deposition of all sorts of filth," a practice that served "to a great extent to mitigate the possible healthfulness of the town." A public meeting took the first step to correct the situation that month, forming a committee "to raise the necessary fund [sic] to build a public water closet, procure some disinfectant, and make such improvements as the expansion of the camp demanded." Overshiner's partner, E. E. Vincent, was one of the committee members.[5]   That the *Print* three years later, in March, 1885, had to campaign for the selection of a new sanitation committee was evidence enough that the people of Calico had not improved their practices to any great extent.[6] Trash continued to pass through back doors and to tumble down the steep slope into Wall Street Canyon, or into Jack Ass Ravine. There, stinking accumulations of refuse grew as unwholesome reminders of the settlers' overriding preoccupation with wresting treasure from the ground. Mule and horse dung piled up in Calico's street, which also reeked of animal urine. There were not enough privies to absorb all of the town's human urine and excrement. Those who walked the paths from the camp to mine bunkhouses a mile or more away might commonly encounter unwelcome evidence of human passage.

Calico always depended on imports from the outside world for its needs, save for livestock raised on the LeFurgey ranch and firewood cut—while it lasted—along the Mojave River. In 1885, when the district's population reached perhaps 3,500, the number and variety of local businesses had grown impressively. The camp was bidding strongly to mature into a town of some proportions. Tents had given way to stone, adobe, and false-fronted board and batten commercial structures and residences. About fifty establishments advertised regularly in the *Print*. There may have been as many as seventy-five active businesses. Deputy Sheriff Joseph Le Cyr announced that "Teaming, Ore Hauling" were specialties. He also ran a livery stable. Mrs. (Annie?) Johnson operated a bakery. R. F. Burgess visited from time to time to provide dental service. There were now three physicians. Dr. Goodenough now advertised himself as a dentist and druggist. Pennsylvania native Dr. Albert Romeo Rhea, a graduate of Western Reserve University, arrived in 1885 and remained through the end of the 1880s and most of the following decade. He delivered most of Calico's babies and acquired extensive mining and land interests, as well. Associated with him was Dr. J. H. Johnson. Hank Mason's Livery and Feed Stable cared for stock. There were a lumber yard, a hay yard, a United States Deputy Surveyor, an assayer, an auction store. Five firms advertised lodgings. Hugh Stevens of general store and borax renown owned one of the last. V. Van Bresen and Seymour Alf provided ICE! ICE! ICE! Bahten & Curry's Pioneer Meat Market provisioned the area with meat. Its owners had since March 1 slaughtered livestock worth between $9,000 and $10,000, including 279 cattle, 80 swine, 140 sheep. Slaughtering occurred thrice weekly, and the meat was delivered at once to town. Purchasers cooked it immediately, to prevent spoilage.

The stage line was still in service in mid-1885. Calico boasted a just-completed Town Hall, erected through the efforts of the community's ladies at a cost of $750. Several stamp mills offered custom milling. There were two dealers in boots and shoes, two in black powder and mining supplies, three purveyors of liquor and cigars, a merchant tailor, an attorney, a Wells, Fargo & Company agent, J. K. Kincaid & Company's General Merchandise, and Kirwyn & Flynn's General Mercantile. Thirsty miners could purchase five-cent beer at Sutcliffe & Quinn, and beverages at Collins and Poieries Saloon, Isaac Noel's Saloon, or any of at least four and perhaps as many as nine other drinking places. All of these offered gambling, and several still housed barbers. Two restaurants publicized their offerings. It is clear, too, that several women were in respectable lines of business. Besides Mrs. Johnson's bakery, there was Mary E. Decky, a milliner; a seamstress; a dancing school; E. H. Moran's laundry; a housewife who offered ice cream made to order; and women also operated at least some of the local lodging houses.[7] Calico never attracted a bank. Merchants cashed checks and extended credit to customers as needed. Wells, Fargo shipped in currency and coin for cashing checks.

After the expansive boom years ended, Calico's population drifted downward. An 1888 directory put the population at only five hundred, identified but sixteen silver mines engaged in sporadic activity, and listed only eighteen other businesses. Still, the full range of merchandise and services usually found in towns of comparable size were available. There was even a stationer-jeweler.[8] Things temporarily improved afterward. A directory for 1889 optimistically asserted that the "various camps [in the Calico district] are on the improve and general good times are confidently expected. The townsite . . . [enjoyed] a daily stage" connecting with trains at Daggett and also at Barstow. "The place has a telephone, telegraph and postoffice [sic] with a daily mail, a hotel and several general stores. The nearest express office" was at Daggett, and, "The newspaper—'The Calico Print'—has been sold and moved away. The town needs a weekly paper." The directory placed the population at "about 800." It listed no businesses, but it did list working inhabitants by name and occupation. Among them were one stage operator, six teamsters, three saloon keepers, three merchants (Hugh Stevens was still one of them), Dr. Rhea, two smiths, two attorneys, one clerk, one "capitalist," an assayer, a produce merchant, a farmer (on the river), three carpenters, one barber, one livery stable operator, one U. S. Deputy Surveyor, one bookkeeper, a postmaster, a clerk, four women identified as widows or landladies, a shoemaker, a tailor, two millers, and a male teacher. Gone were the milliner, seamstress, dance school, baker, three of 1885's lodging places, and four of the saloons. Of the 236 employed persons listed by name and occupation in the directory, only four were females.[9]   With a decline of population had come a loss of occupational opportunities for women. Miners numbered 192, still more than 80 percent of the total work force.

By 1890, the combined population of Barstow, Calico, Daggett, and Hawley was 831, of whom 431 resided in Calico and 277 in Daggett. Passage of the Sherman Act that year prompted a short-lived revival of activity.   The Waterloo mills enlarged their shifts from thirty to two hundred millers, and some seven hundred miners and millers worked in the area. Daggett, however, was emerging as the principal town of the district. Calico's population dwindled gradually and unevenly through the end of the decade, when it stood at perhaps 250 or so. Its businesses dried up as it withered. The failure in 1890 of a San Bernardino bank forced the Norton Brothers Store into bankruptcy. Two years later, in 1892, John R. Lane bought the building and merchandise from Norton Brothers' assignees and entered business. A native of Georgia, he had come to Calico as a teamster. After four years on the desert, he returned to the Peach State to see whether his knowledge of western mining techniques could be put to profitable use in the gold district around Dahlonega. When he concluded that it could not, he traveled back to California. After an interim of farming near Elsinore, he returned in 1890 to Calico and bought the Calico Water Works for $1,500. By maintaining the water works himself and managing it carefully he had been able to pay it off fully and save $2,000 in two years. His acquisition of the store positioned him as Calico's leading, and finally its only, merchant during its declining years. While keeping store he also served as the camp's last Wells, Fargo express agent.[10]

The distinctive characteristics of a mining town shaped Calico's civic life and growth. The proprietors of the town site arranged for it to be surveyed on May 1-3, 1882, as the rush was beginning. Merchant William L[loyd] G[arrison] Soule, became the first postmaster on May 18. The first issue of the *Print* informed the county school commission that there were already in the camp "some twenty five children of age sufficient to entitle them to school privileges." It continued with a respectful request for the formation of a "School District for this portion of the county." The Supervisors of San Bernardino County obliged on October 23, when they divided the Mojave School District and created the Calico School District.[11]

Table 5.1 summarizes the records of the Calico School. Classes began

Table 5.1
Calico School District, 1882-1898

Year	Property Val. (Sch. Tax.)	Pupils	Average Dly. Attend.	Length Of Term	Budget	State & Co. Aid
1882	$ 515.00	58	15	5 months	$ 141.91	$ 162.92
1883	570.00	33	20	7 "	1,373.58	1,072.39
1884	1,275.00	54	25	7 "	1,109.01	1,101.68
1885	500.00	61	34	6.5 "	1,208.59	1,198.99
1886	3,980.00	66	39	9 "	4,106.65	1,177.42
1887	3,980.00	30	19	7 "	1,157.44	1,192.71
1888			31			
1889	3,980.00	40	30	8 "	825.03	840.24
1890	3,980.00	50	33	10 "	1,020.82	1,365.17
1891	2,475.00	41	27	8 "	1,337.54	915.54
1892	2,475.00	30	17	8 "	826.15	840.24
1893			28			
1894	2,325.00	30	22	7 "	672.92	806.04
1895	2,350.00	22	20	8 "	836.59	738.00
1896	2,355.00	21	18	8 "	698.45	763.20
1897	2,355.00	11	5	8 "	692.34	690.00
1898	1,350.00	4	3	n.a.	462.50	523.00

Sources: C. Burton Thrall, Superintendent of Schools, San Bernardino County, personal letter to the author, May 7,1958, from the annual reports of Superintendent of Schools, San Bernardino County, 1882-1883 through 1898-1899; and Alan Baltazar, *Calico*, 59-61, which also contains an Appendix listing teachers by name, and their salaries.

in the Silver King boarding house a few weeks after the formation of the new district. They continued at that site until 1885, when a $3,000 bond issue allowed purchasing a lot and erecting a schoolhouse. The school never grew beyond a single room. Steepled and white-painted, it stood conspicuously at the upper end of Calico Street. The teacher for 1882-1883 was Ella Wagner Soule, the postmaster's wife. Her salary was $135.56. For that sum she taught fifty-eight children, although average daily attendance was only fifteen.

Children attending the Calico School walked in from distances of as far as two miles, from Occidental and Odessa Canyons, over rugged mountain paths. The large bell in the steeple, which echoed far across the desert, began and ended the day. Over the seventeen years of its operation, the school served anywhere from three to sixty-six children in sessions ranging from five to ten months. Average daily attendance varied from three to thirty-nine. Budgets, after a school district was formed, ranged from $462.50 to a high in 1886 of $4,106.65, when the school building was paid for. The school closed permanently on September 6, 1899. Six years later the building was sold and moved to Barstow.[12]

Winning recognition as a legal jurisdiction took longer than securing a school. Almost from its birth Calico employed its own two constables and justices of the peace. All of these held elective office. The camp, however, remained a part of the Belleville Judicial Township for several years. On November 5, 1885, its occupants petitioned the county board of supervisors to constitute a Calico jurisdiction. On that December 8 the board did so, creating the Calico Judicial Township. Establishment of the new entity meant that trials falling within the competence of justices of the peace could occur in Calico, under the watchful attention of its inhabitants. An irregular parallelogram about fifty miles on a side, the township spanned a huge area. Its boundaries extended from Red Butte (the former Nebo Siding, now a part of the United States Marine Corps Supply Depot at Yermo) east to Warm (also known as Zzyzx) Springs on Soda Lake, then north to Tecopa, west to Wingate Canyon, and thence back to the point of origin. The county supervisors reincorporated it back into the Belleville Judicial District on June 20, 1898, when declining population made it unnecessary.[13] Calico enjoyed status as a separate voting precinct for a comparable period, from September 3, 1884, through the election of 1900. Polling took place at the school house. The county commissioners also approved the appointment of fire commissioners, in an action of December 7, 1885.

Provisions for law enforcement, the administration of justice, convenient voting, and instruction for Calico's children were all essential civic

functions.   A consuming preoccupation with the practical concerns of
gaining wealth, or at least with making a living, sharply limited willingness
to expand government services and to pay taxes for them. The Town Hall
originated through private charity, as we have seen. The community never
incorporated. When a proposal for incorporation came up at a town meeting
in February 1885, it was roundly rejected: incorporation was, opponents
believed, too expensive.[14]

Immediate, practical, and local concerns also largely drove political
behavior in Calico. At a time in American history when 80 percent or more
of eligibles registered and voted, Calico's miners were, as a rule, too busy
to do so. In 1884, when the precinct's population probably exceeded two
thousand and was overwhelmingly adult and male, only 250 votes were cast.
Party loyalties inclined toward the Democracy, often by margins of two or
more to one. Where a campaign offered a clear choice between defenders
and critics of mining, voters could cross party lines and cast their ballots for
the former. When the 1884 Congressional contest pitted Republican Henry
Markham, with his ties to Calico, against R. F. Del Valle, Markham came
within seven votes of carrying the precinct. He had, a former Calico
carpenter later reminisced, "one great advantage in being a mining man."
Del Valle lost the election, in part because of his opposition to hydraulic
mining in a state where the mining industry was still strong enough to beat
back farmers trying to end the flooding it caused. In 1896, although Lucy
Lane may have been correct in remembering that there were only two
avowed Republicans in Calico, McKinley drew six votes to fifty-eight for
Bryan. That year's congressional race probably provided a more accurate
measure of relative party strength: the Republican candidate attracted
seventeen votes, the Democratic-Populist fusion nominee, forty-two.

Campaigning at Calico was as lusty as anywhere.   Inhabitants who were
interested in politics displayed the same appetites for parades, campaign
songs, speeches—and heckling and pranks—as their counterparts across the
country. Both Congressional candidates appeared there in 1884. A newly
formed brass band showed its impartiality by performing at rallies for each
of them. The town glee club sang. Miners enthusiastically espoused the
slogan, "The mines made California. Keep the mines going."   Markham
partisans attempted to derail the Del Valle rally by inciting the speaker who
was to introduce him to talk at great length and thus cut severely into his
time.[15]

Work pervaded life in Calico. It was performed in one of the least
hospitable settings in North America, and in an industry notable for the

physical demands it imposed on workers. People employed in the mining industry worked long hours, at ten per day across the week. Their labor was grimy, hard, and dangerous. How grimy an 1884 incident at the Oriental Mill showed. The mill boss was "showing a lady from San Francisco" through the facility. "In due time they arrived at the dump where the ore was dropped from the wagons upon a platform whence it was fed to the stamps. The ore at this mill contained red oxide of iron in such quantity that everyone and everything was coated blood-red from the dust." While they were standing on the mill platform, the lady nearly atop a trap door, the mill boss noticed the door starting to rise. "Knowing that the bin man was about to come through it, and it being impossible to make one's voice heard above the roar of the fifteen . . . stamps doing their dance," the guide took the lady's arm and led her away from the trap door. She turned to see why. Horrified shrieks that overcame "the roar of the machinery" followed. "Framed in the opening," she saw "the bin man's head and torso, striped [sic] to the waist, coated thick with red dust and with rivulets of sweat running through it." With "a respirator (pig snout, we used to call it) and goggles, he was indeed a fearsome sight. . . ."[16]

Miners paid a heavy price for their livings. They performed exhausting work. Some were maimed, and others lost their lives in accidents. Considering the relatively small population of the area, the toll was great enough. Statistics are not an adequate measure of its dimensions. One gains a fuller sense of the tragedy it wrought by turning to events for which records survive. These also graphically catalogued the hazards that lay at every hand. Tom Lenard, a native of Ireland, was found accidentally burned to death in his cabin in 1884. The following year John C. A. McDonald was the victim of an explosion in the Bismarck Mine. While he was inspecting a charge, it detonated, breaking a leg, mangling his arms, and blowing out his eyes. He died two hours later. Malcolm McLeod fell to his death down chute number three from the Silver King's fifth level on January 25,1886. On May 13,1888, George S. Johnston came to his death "by falling over a precipice about one mile east of the Waterloo mine . . . ." The following February a mule kick dispatched Constable John M. McCulloch. Early in 1891 a ceiling fall buried James McGowan, only sixteen years old, in the Waterloo Mine. Searchers never recovered his body. That same year on the day after Christmas Daniel Malloy died accidentally by falling off a bluff on the trail between Calico and East Calico and "striking on his head & breaking his neck . . . ." A cave-in took W.G. English, in the Oriental No. 2 Mine, in mid-1895. In 1899 two miners succumbed to "Accidental asphyxiation . . ." in the Desert King Mine. A cave-in claimed yet another miner after the turn of the century.

Those who escaped accidents were by no means free of risks. Disappointment, isolation, gambling losses, alcoholism, and depression resulted in at least a half dozen suicides. Self-inflicted gunshot wounds to the head were the preferred method of self destruction. At least one miner hanged himself in his cabin. Another died in a mine by "[rat] poison administered by his own hand." There is a story that notorious drunk John "Jack" Dent came to his end, as he wished, in a drinking spree that saw him consume more than one hundred shots of whisky, on the July 4, 1893. The Calico cemetery record lists the cause of death as "alcoholism," which lends support to the tale. The coroner's inquest, however, placed his end in January, 1884 and attributed it to "A Revolver shot in his own hands Either Accidental or Intentionly."[17]

If they escaped accidental injury or death, and did not take their own lives, Calico's miners were subject to the same health hazards that confronted all of the people of the district. Many of these originated in the same inadequate sanitation that stirred the *Calico Print* to editorial comment from time to time. Records of causes of death for the 130 souls buried in the Calico cemetery are far from complete. Those that survive cannot be wholly trusted. Given the state of contemporary medicine and diagnostic tools, neither coroners' juries nor local physicians could always determine causes of death. Too often, coroners' inquests could say no more than that an individual died "by natural causes," or that "we have no means of knowing the cause of . . . death." For forty-three of those slumbering in the cemetery who lived in Calico during its heyday, we have no indication of the reason for death. At least four of the ten known children, two of them stillborn, who are buried there died for reasons unknown. There are no birth dates for another seventeen, some of whom were likely children.

Diseases that have long since ceased to be serious threats in this country were familiar visitors to Calico. Diphtheria took at least one life; typhoid fever two in 1885; and diarrhea, inflamed bowels, or cholera (possibly amoebic dysentery?), four. Pneumonia carried off no less than seven, some victims suffering as well from consumption (tuberculosis). There were at least four major outbreaks of typhoid fever, which was more or less endemic there throughout Calico's existence. The first, accompanied by diphtheria, occurred in the summer of 1882. Another, described by some writers as "la grippe" or influenza, occurred in 1883. The disease struck again in 1885. Sufferers then included four-year-old Mary Bell "Minnie" Whitfield, who died on April 29 after a "five day sickness." Lucy Lane was among those stricken in the fall of 1892. Fortunately, she recovered. When epidemics raged, carpenters used rough lumber to throw crude coffins together, "as it took too long by freight teams for Undertakers supplies to reach Calico from San Bernardino." Josephine A Miller, the wife of storekeeper Joseph Moore Miller, lined them with black Calico cloth, fastened with brass headed tacks.[18]

What compensations and rewards did Calico offer to offset the hazards, hostile desert environment, and hard work that it imposed? There were several. The pay was comparatively good. Mine foremen initially earned $5 a day, miners $4, above-ground workers, $3. Even in the mid-1880s, when scales had fallen respectively by a dollar, they were at or above the California average. Boss carpenters at first received $10, later, $8. The prevailing national rate for manufacturing workers at the time was only $425 per year.[19]

From their earnings silver miners, like their fellows at Borate and vicinity mill workers, could expect to pay seventy-five cents to a dollar a day for room and board if they stayed at a company bunkhouse. If they did not, they could rent rooms in any of several local hotels and rooming houses, some providing board, some not, for comparable rates. Those who occupied their own cabins and cooked for themselves trudged twice a week to one of Calico's general stores to buy groceries and other supplies. The trip involved carrying an empty burlap bag for their purchases. If it were made after dark, shoppers also had to carry a coal oil lantern to cast a flickering light along the way. On the return trek, the men slung their loaded gunny sacks over a shoulder, grasping them with one hand while carrying their lanterns in the other. Those who walked in from East Calico faced the extra challenge of a difficult trail. Where families lived in homes in town, wives generally walked to the store whenever necessary.

For their money, residents of Calico could obtain essentially all of the supplies they needed without leaving town. Their desert location placed fresh fruits and vegetables at a premium. Even these could be obtained in limited quantities. "Pa" Levi Pennington and his wife, who farmed a few miles up the river from Barstow at what is now known as Hinkley, brought in fresh fruits and vegetables in season once a week to sell at "fancy prices." A manuscript account book from one of Calico's stores offers a rare glimpse at prices and purchasing habits, as is shown in Table 5.2. One can also discover from this tattered volume that overalls sold for eighty five cents, whisky for $5 a gallon and brandy for $4, cigarettes for ten cents a package, a box of salted cod fish for $5, a can of assorted pie fruit for $5, and a case of tinned corned beef for $2.60. General merchants and grocers carried

Table 5.2
Commodity Prices in Calico

W. M. Garrett		Stephen Rowe		
6 # rice	$ .50	13 #	ham	$2.34
3 bars soap	.25	50 #	flour	1.85
1 # tea	.50	1 #	G&B Tea	.75
4 # arabian coffee	1.35	5	cans milk	1.00
25 # spuds	.75	11 #	sugar	1.00
12 # onion	.50	2	cans strawberry jam	.50
22 # sugar	2.00	1	Pa[ckage] Cocoanut	.25
1 can B[aking]	.55	1	Bot. Ketchup	.35
Powder	25	5	cans Lard	.65
1 box pepper	1.00	1	can Pepper	.25
6 cans corn	.90	3	cans tomatoes	.50
2 doz eggs	1.85	1 #	B[aking] Powder	.55
50 # flour	.70	2 #	Dried Peas	.25
1 roll butter	1.17	1	Jar Mustard	.20
6 1/2# bacon	1.00	1	Pa[ckage] stove polish	.10
5 cans Eagle Milk	1.00	1	doz. eggs	.45
6 cans Highland	.25	1 #	white beans	.20
3 # apples	.80	2 #	sage	.25
Lantern	1.00	2	Pa[ckages] starch	.25
1 Stew Pot	1.50	6	bars soap	.50
1 wire clothes line	.50	1	can Ginger	.30
1 chicken	.65	5 #	Honey	3.50
. . . .	. . .	1	pr. Shoes	3.50
		1	cap	.85

Source: Ledger book from a Calico general store—probably's Lane's General Mercantile, lent to the author by Lucile Coke, formerly of Yermo, California. Entries are for the date of December 31, 1892.

ample stocks of provisions and at prices that made them affordable.

Operators of family farms and residents of more favorably situated towns and cities in the United States enjoyed an even greater range of dietary choices in season. The people of Calico nevertheless shared in the abundance that set this country apart from the rest of the world. They purchased in quantity such staples as flour, rice, potatoes, onions, and sugar. Steady traffic in baking powder pointed to the importance of domestic baking. Locals regularly consumed coffee, tea, and canned milk. Fresh eggs were no novelty, cured ham was always for sale, and canned and dried vegetables could be purchased easily. Condiments, including spices, seasonings, sweeteners such as honey, and preserves added flavor to meals. Tables sagged under the heavy burdens of food necessary to satisfy hearty miners' and millers' appetites. Purchases of soap, blueing, starch, and the like showed that clean and pressed clothing were sought after even in a late nineteenth- century Mojave Desert silver and borax camp.[20]

As quickly as possible, new arrivals in Calico attempted to make it like the towns that they had known while living in longer-established regions. Despite the difficulties involved in importing lumber, by 1883 frame buildings were common. Coal-burning kitchen stoves heated food. Comfortable furnishings were common, even in rooming and boarding houses. Many families had by the mid-1880s built multiple-bedroom houses, some of stone and mortar, or of puddled mud created by mixing water with earth excavated from basements. At least one Chinese, meanwhile, constructed a cabin of used kerosene cans. Evaporative coolers, made by placing a perforated water-filled container such that the water would drip on to burlap or some similar material placed around a box containing food items that needed to be protected from excessive heat, were extensively employed. Some families, while still living in tents, had them. Photographs, decorative objects, ubiquitous Victorian knick-knacks, good China and silver, curtains, even elegant candle sconces decorated the nicer homes. Apparently some who abandoned Calico expected to return. When the caved-in basements of their former homes were excavated, diggers found, among other things, barrels filled with carefully packed China and glassware. Stores, restaurants, offices, and saloons boasted comparable appointments, including up-to-date shelving and counters, even fine redwood and hardwood bars and elegant mirrors.

Arid desert conditions rapidly drew the moisture out of wood. It quickly became tinder dry. As a result, fire was a constant danger. After a blaze swept through Calico in 1884, it was "rapidly rebuilt, this time with good, substantial structures, many of them of stone to act as firebreaks in event of a recurrence. "But," the California State Mineralogist noted, "unfortunately in one year from the date of the first burning, a second conflagration laid the town in ashes." Calico rebuilt again, and again with more substantial structures. Its appearance was that of a sizeable and flourishing mining community until the much greater fire of September 1887 destroyed 135 structures. Even with piped water, the absence of an organized fire company and of anything resembling real fire fighting equipment made a desperate situation entirely hopeless. Lucy Lane "learned the cause of the fire" years later, from Eugenia Porter. While Porter was curling her hair for a dance, the pet goat of her brother entered her room, "saw his reflection [in the mirror] . . . and made a lunge" overturning the coal oil lamp on her dresser. Flames shot up immediately. The goat "was cremated," but Eugenia escaped. "She never had the courage to tell her parents what caused the fire." The expansive years were over. Nevertheless, residents once more repaired the damage and resumed normal lives, with their satisfactions.[21]

Those satisfactions included the amusements that pervaded mostly male mining camps in the American West. Miners, millers, surface workers, and others could wash the desert dust down their throats with beer or stronger drink at any of seven saloons. They could also eat, and, more importantly, gamble at these places. The game of choice was poker, but other card games could be found. By 1885, there may have been as many as thirty professional gamblers seated at tables in Calico's saloons, ready to oblige any man willing, or foolish enough, to risk his stakes. Clouds of cigar smoke filled these establishments with a reeking blue haze, and the clinking sounds of bar pianos provided a raucous musical backdrop. Under the same ownership as most of the saloons, and usually attached to them or next to them, were the dance halls. The saloons, when first built, were at the lower end of the camp's street. With growth, the *Print* related early in 1885, "so many residences have been built below them that . . . [they] are almost in the center of town."

Prostitution flourished in Calico as in virtually every Western mining camp. Those engaged in it pursued one of a small number of occupations (outside of the home) open to many women. The town apparently had neither high-class bordellos catering to an exclusive and prosperous clientele, or, at the opposite end of the social hierarchy within that ancient trade, occupants of cribs, or streetwalkers. Instead, these busy "soiled doves" democratically hustled their services in dance halls to working class customers. How many of them there were cannot now be determined, although Mary "Kitty" Smith is remembered as the owner of one of the establishments. We have seen that sixteen were arrested from one dance hall early in 1885, when patrons complained of being robbed. At that time, the Calico Mining District's population was around 3,500, and the town itself probably harbored 1,200 or so. If brothels were attached to only three of the seven saloons, and each sheltered around twelve to sixteen women as did the one at which the arrests were made, then forty to fifty prostitutes were at work. There could have been twice as many, but certainly not fewer than three dozen. In 1896, the accounts ledger at Lane's Mercantile still listed the names of three of them.

The respectable people of the town treated Calico's prostitutes with the ambiguity combining tolerance, jocularity, disapproval, and distaste, that was customary in contemporary America. However sizeable the demand for their services, however necessary their presence might seem in an overwhelmingly male mining camp, they were degraded. As late as 1896, when declining mining and population had significantly reduced their numbers, they still were obliged to patronize "their own Chinese laundry" and keep to themselves. One old-timer later wrote that they "undoubtedly were" "tough cases." They "smoked cigarettes, drank liquor, and some of them swore," but he never saw any do so on the street and never heard any utter an "unladylike" word while riding in their presence on the stage to Daggett. They were never fully a part of local society. They lived and worked always at its margins.[22]

Those seeking more wholesome amusement could select from a variety of options. The simplest was whiling away the time, perhaps swapping stories over an evening meal or fire. Immigrants to Calico promptly recreated the range of male social organizations and activities that they had known in the East, or in other mining communities. All of these emphasized the masculine character of the town. The Masons, Odd-Fellows, and Democratic and Republican clubs were inevitable features of the social scene. By 1885 a brass band, which knew only one tune when it performed for visiting candidates for state office that year, and a men's glee club, had also formed. Greater excitement occasionally beckoned, too. In March, 1885, the *Print* notified readers, "A glove contest to the finish will take place at the Town Hall of Calico . . . for a purse of $100 and gate receipts, between Dan Connor, of Boston, and Frank Smith, of Chicago. London prize ring rules to govern. . . . To commence at 8 sharp."

Efforts to reproduce locally all of the civilized amenities did not lag, although its support never extended very far beyond the wives of merchants, professionals, and mine and mill superintendents, and their compliant husbands. When Calico was in full bloom, in 1885, it boasted a Literary Society, which stood at the pinnacle of the local social scale. This group met weekly, for orations, plays, debates, readings, discussions, book reviews, and discussion of the great issues of the day. Always interested in federal financial policy, it not surprisingly resolved on one occasion that "the coinage of silver should not be suspended, so President [Grover] Cleveland will be compelled to change his policy on that subject." Somehow he failed to hear of this pronouncement and continued unswervingly on a conservative fiscal course. There were also a Debating Club, a Ladies' Whist Club, and opportunities for outings and picnics at Fish Ponds, the LeFurgey Ranch, at Sue Falls in Wall Street Canyon and elsewhere, as well as the sort of round-robin calling at home that families of the time enjoyed. During the scorching days of June through September, many of Calico's leading families retreated to seashore cottages they had bought or built in Oceanside. With outside work close to impossible, all laborers, carpenters, teamsters, and others who could do so retreated, as desert folk still say, "down below," to the coastal valleys where more moderate temperatures prevailed.

Preachers began to proclaim the Gospel in Calico as early as October 15,1881, when the Reverend Charles Shelley conducted a service in the store of Alfred James for a congregation of twenty gentlemen, ladies, and children. The occasion seemed to the *Print* another important moment in Calico's life. Editor Overshiner endorsed Shelley's arrival, hoped that he would return, and predicted that the camp's people would "ere long move in the matter to obtain a suitable building for holding religious services." Shelley was still visiting three years later. The Reverend D. McCunn, who had a regular appointment at Daggett, Mojave, and Needles, had joined him, probably to celebrate mass with Roman Catholics. In mid-1885 he was reassigned. That same year Father Elias Cook, a Catholic, arrived as a missionary, probably to succeed McCunn. Once completed, the Town Hall became the focal point for worship. It was standard practice for Roman Catholic and Protestant clergymen to officiate on alternate Sundays. There was even a wheezing pump organ with which to accompany the singing. Accounts conflict as to the depth of piety in the remote desert town. One reminiscence recounted how a Cornish miner responded favorably to an evangelist until the latter prayed. When asked what was wrong with the prayer he replied, "Well, he maket long prayer and asket for *everything*, then at end tellet Lord to do just as He damn please about it, he don't care." He had never encountered the petition, *"Nevertheless,* not my will, but *thine* be done." An 1896 visitor from San Francisco claimed that Calico hazed all clergymen, so that while many came, none stayed. Long time residents, in contrast, remembered regular worship services. It is not unlikely that the same civic spirit that led Calico's respectable ladies to provide for the construction of the Town Hall always provided a core of committed worshipers, whatever the temperaments of the mine workers.[23]

After roads reached East Calico and the bunkhouses and the ore bins of all the principal mines in the Calicos, no miner was too remote to enjoy either reasonable access to the attractions of town or to the conveniences that were generally available at the time. Beyond the point where water pipes ended, water wagons made deliveries to keep local barrels full, still at a cost of four or five cents a gallon. Town was within no more than an

View of Calico from the Silver King Mine, ca. 1890. *Photo courtesy Mojave River Valley Museum.*

Group of Miners in front of Unidentified Store. Date Unknown. *Photo courtesy Mojave River Valley Museum.*

Sheriff John C. King, ca. 1895–1900. *Photo courtesy Mojave River Valley Museum.*

Dorsey, the Mail Dog. *Photo courtesy Mojave River Valley Museum.*

hour's walk. Either way, The stage connected with Daggett in no more than an hour more. Either way, a shave and a bath a week were possible, and normal. Even East Calico enjoyed mail service. W. L. G. Soule vacated the position of postmaster in October 1885. His partner in business, Everet E. "Bill" Stacy, with whom he had built the Stone Front Building after fire consumed the first post office, succeeded him for four years. Stacey's brother, Alwin, operated a store and post office at the Occidental Mine in East Calico. The two had a contract to deliver the mail to East Calico. One cold morning early that year Everet found a stray collie shivering on the store doorstep and took him in. Before long, with an initial "few lashes of the whip" followed by rewards of food and kindness, they had trained the dog to carry the mail between Calico and East Calico. The dog, renamed from "Jack" to "Dorsey," did so for about a year, using specially designed saddle bags, and leather booties to protect his feet from the sharp stones on the trail. The Staceys gave him to the then owner of the Bismarck Mine, W. W. Stow, in February 1886. A Stow associate took Dorsey to Stow's home in San Francisco, where the dog lived out his days in retirement.[24]

Anti-Chinese sentiment never completely died out. In time some forty Chinese lived beyond Jack Ass Gulch just east of the bench on which most of Calico stood. To avoid having to climb down and then back up the sides of the gully, they built a small bridge between their quarters and town. Yung Hen was head man of the local Chinese. As Teong Kee, he owned restaurants and stores; he grubstaked a number of miners and carried others on account, earning considerable respect as a result. Several operated hand laundries. The Mechams recounted one violent incident that erupted after a white lost to a Chinese at a game of chance in one of the saloons, in 1887. The white rallied friends to attack Chinatown, but the mob lost heart after batteries of flatirons, rocks, shingles, and other types of debris repulsed two attempts to invade by way of the bridge. When compared with far more lethal confrontations that occurred elsewhere, this seemed a modest enough encounter. At that, the Mechams said that Sino-American relations in Calico improved considerably after the incident. There were apparently no further attempts at mob violence. J. R. Lane's day book still listed eight Chinese residents as late as 1896.[25]

How violent, then, was life in Calico? The mother of teen-aged Herman Mellen, upon learning that he was to accompany his father to do carpentry work at Calico in the fall of 1882 exclaimed, "What, Take that boy, only fifteen, into that wild mining camp, among those wild miners? No! NO!" There is no doubt that Calico was a hard–drinking town. One store averaged

$53 per day for liquor, grossing $1,490 in February 1885 alone for liquor sales at the low prices of the time. But Mellen himself many years later wrote that while carrying guns was very common in Calico, the population was remarkably peaceable. We "were," he said, "quite law-abiding. Though almost everyone maintained his own standing in the camp without the aid of officials, it was done also without the use of force." The unwritten principle "growing out of these conditions was based upon mutual respect, and honesty." Lucy Lane averred that "not having a jail . . . [Calico] seemed to be a more law abiding town than many earlier gold camps . . . ." She added that there "were few gun fights and people were generally law-abiding citizens . . . ." Historian Remi Nadeau was in a good position to add his own incisive comments. Named for a great-great-grandfather who was Southern California's foremost freighter and one of the key figures in the development of Los Angeles during the 1870s and 1880s, he drew on family records to arrive at the same conclusion. Such comments have become the conventional wisdom.[26]

Although fire, time, and the elements have destroyed much of the record, enough remains to provide a glimpse at the level of violence that obtained in the Calico district while it was active. That glimpse is revealing. Even allowing for the almost complete disappearance of records of the local justice courts, and thus of misdemeanors, it is clear that Calico was far from immune to crime and violent behavior. The narrow escape from an armed showdown between employees of the Garfield and the Occidental Mines in February 1885, the egg attack at the May Day Ball later that year, and the attempted mob invasion of Calico's Chinese quarter have already received attention. None of them came to much. Other incidents were more serious.

One of the graves in the Calico cemetery contains the remains of "Blackie" Scroggins. Scroggins apparently was hanged on May 1,1882, for claim jumping. There is reason to believe that he was not the only person buried there to die at the end of a rope. Wes Wescott, whose marker indicates birth in 1871 and death in 1889, may have been hanged for the same offense and also without benefit of a formal trial. The four original owners of the Burning Moscow Mine fell victim to their own greed and jealousy in a series of fatal encounters. On June 8,1882, John A. Taylor, characterized as a quarrelsome drunk, shot and killed his cousin Johan August Peterson in San Bernardino after several days of drinking and fighting. He then turned his gun on himself, firing his last bullet into his "left nipple" just as Peterson staggered from the street to the porch of their hotel and collapsed, dead. That same year John "Banjo Bob" Whitefield, merchant and constable in Calico, stabbed Artemas [Hieronymous] Hartman.

Thinking he had killed Hartman, he shot himself to death while released from jail on bail. Hartman survived, only to meet a violent death years later while resisting arrest.[27]

The following year another fatal gunfight flared. This one took place in Calico, rather than between residents who happened temporarily to be staying elsewhere as had been the case with Taylor and Peterson. An argument erupted in John Ackerman's Saloon between miners John T. Sullivan and self-described "bad man from Bodie" John J. Williams on April 19,1883. Sullivan said he would kill Williams. The two stepped outside where the latter drew his pistol and fired two shots, one passing through the former's left eye and exiting the back of his head. He died minutes later. A trial in San Bernardino resulted in Williams' release with a finding that he had acted in self-defense. Perhaps so, but he was also a bad egg. Not long after, he entered a local saloon, placed his pistol on the bar, and demanded drinks. He downed two without paying, then slapped the bar tender when he was told he could have no more unless he paid up. When he angrily attempted to push into another saloon across the street soon after, the forewarned barkeeper shot and killed him.[28]

It was in October of the next year that the *Print* noted with satisfaction the killing of John Doe at the Pastime Saloon. Then two days before Christmas in 1884, an unknown attacker blew Reese Nichols out of this world, probably as a result of a dispute over a mine. In February 1885, William E. Curry shot and killed William Deegan as the latter was breaking into his home. That April a potentially murderous assault took place when a drunken James Jordan stabbed Pat O'Day in the back and slashed his head with a butcher knife in Collins and Poierie's Saloon. The local justice of the peace found cause to charge Jordan with assault with intent to commit murder. When tried in San Bernardino, Jordan pleaded guilty to a reduced charge of simple assault and was fined $75. Thomas Felis was slain on May 23,1885.[29]

There was at least one further shooting, in 1886, arising from a dispute over a mine. Ms. Annie Kline (Rickhert) Townsend had earlier filed on two silver claims, the Alhambra and the Golconda, and then granted options on them to H. S. Tobler. Tobler continued to work them after the options expired and without paying. When she ordered him to leave the property, he merely glanced up at her and grinned while continuing to work in the shaft. She aimed her weapon and fired, wounding him, and he brought charges. A court exonerated her.[30] The year 1889 began with the arrest in mid-January of Orrie Parker for stealing a horse. Sent to the San Bernardino jail, he escaped a day later. He was not seen again. Just days later Justice of the

Peace H. B. Gregory found "sufficient cause" to believe that Jim Tye had assaulted Charlie Sing, a Chinese, "with intent to commit murder by striking . . . [him] with an iron bar about two feet long and by shooting at . . . Sing with a pistol." The case went to trial in San Bernardino, where Tye was convicted of assault. The same year Gong Nil, one of Sing's countrymen, was arrested in Calico for the murder of a compatriot. On September 10 Harry Dodson, a former millman for the Runover Company, robbed Runover Mine Superintendent James Patterson of a payroll of $4,395. Patterson composed a posse consisting of saloon owner John Ackerman, an Indian tracker, Tecopa John, and himself; and set out in pursuit. They caught up with Dodson on the next day at Coyote Hole (Wells), and Patterson killed him in a gunfight. They brought the body back to Calico, where it was buried in the cemetery.[31] The last gunfight at Calico of which we have knowledge took place in 1896. Early in the morning of May 17, after an all-night card game, an argument broke out at Dickerson and Mosely's Saloon. Unemployed Los Angeles mining broker Albert P. Roland drew a pistol in an attempt to restore order. Professional gambler Edward P. Scollard pulled out a knife and advanced on Roland. Following a heated exchange, Scollard drew a pistol and shot Roland in the chest. The broker died soon after, and a court on July 17,1896, found Scollard guilty of manslaughter, sentencing him to seven years in San Quentin prison.

The tally, incomplete as it is, is grim enough. Three deaths associated with the Burning Moscow, two probable lynchings for claim jumping, at least six murders, one housebreaker killed, one known incident of horse thievery, one payroll robbery that ended fatally, one conviction for manslaughter, one shooting in defense of a mine, and two trials for assault with intent to commit murder that resulted in convictions on lesser charges. Had more copies of the *Calico Print* survived, the picture might become more sobering. At that, the possibility of homicide was always close to the surface. The prospect of violence loomed large enough to challenge the notion that the camp was an unusually quiet one even though pioneers later recalled that it was. The incidence of murder in Calico, 1882-1900, was comparable with those that Robert Dykstra discovered in his study of Abilene, Ellsworth, Wichita, Dodge City, and Caldwell, Kansas when they were in their heyday as cattle towns. None was as lawless as the misconceptions of later generations maintained, none a place of Edenic peace. Violent deaths averaged about 1.5 per town per year. Incomplete surviving records hint that they may have numbered 1.0 to 1.5 per year in Calico, too. Local authorities were as a rule able to keep order in Calico as well as they were in countless frontier and interior communities.[32] That was not as remarkable as it might seem. The desert yielded its riches grudgingly. Hard, continuous work was required if the mines were to pay and the district to thrive. Purposeful effort was also the price required to introduce and preserve the essential elements of civilized existence. The people of Calico knew as much. They had no desire to escape from civilization. They understood that order must be maintained if the needed work were to be accomplished and their lives were to be tolerable.

This chapter took as its point of departure a mural representing "Saturday Night in Calico, 1881." Despite its anachronisms, inaccuracies, and glamorization, it turns out that we cannot fault the mural in one sense. It did, whether knowingly or not, point toward some important truths. It captured the masculinity, the boisterousness, the roughness, the sheer energy, even the occasional colorful irruptions of play, that to varying degrees characterized life there. In portraying the camp in larger-than-life terms, it also hinted at a significant heroic quality. This proved to be incisive. Given the very real constraints that bounded human experience in Calico, its inhabitants' achievements were notable. Local mines could not pour out treasure to rival the wealth that streamed from the Comstock Lode in Virginia City, or from the Black Hills, or from Leadville, or from Cripple Creek, or any of a number of other vastly richer centers. The local population never neared the fifteen, twenty, or twenty-five thousand or more of those places. Nevertheless, Calico was an active center for a quarter century, when borax is considered along with silver. Rude frontier settlement it was not. Its residents approached the standards of living and cultural life that prevailed in many other mining and industrial communities of the time. They earned livings and reproduced the economic, social, and political institutions that characterized town life. They made a town. Some of them brought families. Others married. Children were born. The infirmities of age took some of the elderly. The forebearance and matter-of-fact resoluteness of Calico's people in going about their lives represented a quiet, unobtrusive kind of heroism. If the story of their shared life is memorable, it is most so in these terms. Calico's settlers were agents of civilization, even if at its more remote edges. That they succeeded so well comments favorably on their determination even in their unlikely location.

NOTES

1. The mural, by Paul V. Klieben, housed in the Calico Saloon, Ghost Town, Knott's Berry Farm, Buena Park, is printed on the back cover of Anonymous [Walter Knott], *Calico* (Buena Park: Knott's Berry Farm, 1952).

2. Quotation, Mellen, "Reminiscences," 348. See also Herman F. Mellen, "We Called Them 'Cousin Jacks,'" *Calico Print*, 6 (December, 1950), 2; Great Register of Voters," Calico Precinct, 1882-1890, San Bernardino County Archives.

3. Quotations, stage line, *Calico Print*, July 8, 20, October 21,1882; author's interview with Lucy B. Lane, March 28,1956; Lane, *Memories*, 28-30; Remi Nadeau, *The Ghost Towns of California* (Los Angeles, 1955), 59.

4. W. H. Storms, "San Bernardino County," *Eleventh Report of the State Mineralogist*, 337-69, and *passim*;   F. B. Weeks, "*Bismarck Mine*, Calico Mining District, San Bernardino Co., California" (unpublished geological survey of the Bismarck group of mines at Calico, lent to the author by J. T. Weakely, Los Angeles, undated); *Calico Print*, July 20,1882; Lane, *Memories*, 15.

5. *Calico Print*, July 8, 20, 27,1882.

6. *Calico Print*, March 8,1885.

7. *Calico Print*, February - May 31,1885; Lane interview; for women's opportunities, Sandra L. Myers, *Westering Women and the Frontier Experience 1800-1915* (Albuquerque: University of New Mexico Press, 1982); Paul, *The Far West*, 123-24, 296-97 and *passim*.

8. R. L. Polk & Co., *California State Gazetteer and Business Directory. 1888* (San Francisco: R. L. Polk & Co., 1888), 181.

9. Walker, Charles E., John Flagg, and W. R. McIntosh, *McIntosh, Flagg & Walker's San Bernardino City and County Directory* (San Bernardino, Cal.:   Flagg & Walker, Printers and Binders, 1889), 9-13.

10. Lane, *Memories*, 20, 21, 25, and n. 41; De Groot, "San Bernardino County—Its Mountains Plains and Valleys," *Tenth Annual Report*, 518-533; United States, Census Office, *Compendium of the Eleventh Census of the United States: 1890. Part I.—Population*, 1 (Washington: Government Printing Office, 1892) 73. Calico's Wells, Fargo agents were merchants J. K. Kincaid & Co.; 1883-1885, W. A. Sharp; 1885-1887; R. J. Humphreys, 1887-1892; and Lane, from 1892.

11. *Calico Print*, July 8,1882; San Bernardino County Supervisors, *Record Books*, C (unpublished manuscript, October 23,1882), 389, San Bernardino County Archives.

12. As the table indicates, records for some years were incomplete. Sources for table: C. Burton Thrall, Superintendent of Schools, San Bernardino County, personal letter to the author, May 7,1958, from annual reports of Superintendent of Schools, San Bernardino County, 1882-1883 through 1898-1899;   Baltazar, *Calico*, 59-61, and Appendix III, which lists Calico's teachers and their monthly salaries. Salaries ranged from $75 to $100 per month. About half the time instructors were male, half the time, female. Terms of service rarely exceeded two years. In 1898 Calico's property carried an assessed valuation, for purposes of county taxation, of $41,822. San Bernardino, with a population of about 10,000, say eighty times that of Calico, contained property valued at $3.126 million.

13. Supervisors, *Record Books*, D (September 2,1884, December 8,1885), 96, 296.

14. Supervisors, *Record Books*, D (September 3,1884, December 7,1885), 101ff, 111 (voting precinct), 289 (fire commissioners), E, F, G, I, J (November 14,1898), 244-49. Volume K is missing. For incorporation, *Calico Print*, February 8,1885.

15. Supervisors, *Record Books*, C (1882), 394-95; D (1884), 146-62; D (1886), 432-50; E (1888), 332-50; F (1890), 312-31; G (1892), 387-408; I(1894), 1-14; I (1896), 258-61; J (1898), 244-49; William N. Davis, Jr., Historian, California State Archives, personal letter to the author, November 19,1957; Walter V. Combs, Registrar of Voters, San Bernardino County, personal letter to the author, November 22,1957; and for the 1884

Congressional race in Calico, Mellen, "Reminiscences," 354-56, quoted, 355.

16. Mellen, "Reminiscences," quoted 251-52.

17. Coroner's inquests, Tom Lenard, November 30,1884; George S. Johnston, May 18,1888; Daniel Malloy, December 26,1891; John Burgess and William Marion Medlin October 19,1899;   Robert G. Williams, "CALICO CEMETERY" (unpublished manuscript, compiled 1971-1992); coroner's inquests, John Dent, January 6,1884, J. J. Spainhour, September 27,1885, James Hubbard, January 20,1887, William Dickinson, March 18,1887, Philip Hartoin, January 27,1793; "Burial and Removal Permits [Calico Cemetery]" (unpublished manuscript excerpted from coroner's records, County of San Bernardino); all San Bernardino County Archives.

18. Quotation, Lucy B. Lane, personal letter to the author, May 1958. For typhoid, Lane, *Memories*, 3, 25 and 26, typhoid pneumonia, 19, diphtheria, 14; "la grippe," Mellen, "Reminiscences," 119.

19. United States, Census Office, *Eleventh Census of the United States: 1890*, 7 (Washington: Government Printing Office, 1892), 35;   Albert Rees, *Real Wages in Manufacturing, 1890-1914* (Princeton: Princeton University Press, 1961), 33; Paul Howard Douglas, *Real Wages in the United States, 1860-1914* (Boston: Houghton Mifflin Company, 1934); United States, Bureau of the Census, *Historical Statistics . . . to 1957*, 91, 383.

20. I am indebted to Lucille Coke, formerly of Yermo, California, who discovered this ledger book and graciously lent it to me. The entries are for December 31,1892. The store is unidentified. Given the date of the entries and that on which John R. Lane became a merchant, it is probable that the volume comes from his store.

21. Irelan, *Eighth Report*, 215; *San Francisco Chronicle*, September 5, 11,1887; Lane, *Memories*, 40; Baltazar, *Calico*, Appendix I.

22. Quotations, *Calico Print*, February 22,1885; Mellen, "Reminiscences," 363; Lucy B. Lane, personal letter to the author, April 30,1958.   Perspective: Myers, *Westering Women*, 254-56, 347-48; Anne M. Butler, *Daughters of Joy, Sisters of Misery: Prostitutes in the American West, 1865-90* (Urbana: University of Illinois Press, 1985).   In what appears to be a completely unfounded bit of puffery Larry and Lucille Coke in their 1940 *Calico* claimed that Calico's most notorious woman of the evening was "Diamond Lil," a figure unnamed in standard references and about whom Lucy Lane remarked tartly, "I never heard of Diamond Lil." Writer's interview with Lucy Lane, July 4,1961.

23. Quotations, boxing match, *Calico Print*, March 8,1885; federal fiscal policy, March 22,1885; first worship services, October 21,1882; prayer, Mellen, "Reminiscences," 248; and author's interview with Lucy B. Lane, March 28,1956.

24. Virtually everything that has been written about Calico refers to Jack/Dorsey, whose photograph is probably the best-known picture to survive from old Calico. The first printed reference is "Jack the Mail Dog," *Calico Print*, May 10,1885; while the *San Bernardino Index*, February 27,1886; reports Dorsey's retirement. Lane, *Memories*, 13, and notes 8, 25, and 26 provide further information. Editor Alan Baltazar in note 26 adds that in the 1970s Walt Disney Productions made a film about Dorsey, "Go West, Young Dog."

25. See Mecham's account in *San Bernardino Sun-Telegram*, November 2,1957; Mellen, "Reminiscences," 357-58; Lucy B. Lane, personal letter to the author, April 30,1958; and Baltazar, *Calico*, especially 45, 44.

26. *Calico Print*, July 8,1882; Mellen, "Reminiscences," quoted 107, 362-63; *Calico Print*, March 8,1885; Lucy B. Lane, personal letter to the author, January 6,1965, and author's interview with, July 4,1961; Remi Nadeau, "Old Calico: Model Ghost Town," *Ghost Towns of California* (Los Angeles: The Ward Ritchie Press, 1955), 59-61.

27. *Calico Print*, July 8,1882; *San Francisco Chronicle*, June 9,1882; Williams, "CALICO CEMETERY." For Hartman's death, Baltazar, *Calico*, 45.

28. Coroner's inquest, John T. Sullivan, April 19,1883; *The People of the State of California vs. John J. Williams, Defendant*, 534 Superior Court, County of San Bernardino (1883); both San Bernardino County Archives; Baltazar, *Calico*, 49, 52.

29. Williams, "CALICO CEMETERY," *Calico Print*, October 21,1884, May 10, 24, 1885.

30. *The People of the State of California vs. Annie Kline Townsend, Defendant*, 1433 Superior Court, County of San Bernardino (1887), San Bernardino County Archives.

31. Coroner's inquest, Harry Dodson, September 12,1889, San Bernardino County Archives; for Townsend, Baltazar, *Calico*, 53, 54; Orrie Parker, 47, 54, 55; Gong Nil, 44, 45; *People of the State of California vs. Jim Tye, Defendant*, Justice Court, Calico Township, January 24,1889; *People of the State of California vs. Jim Tye, Defendant*, 2383 Superior Court, County of San Bernardino (1889), both San Bernardino County Archives.

32. Robert Dykstra, *The Cattle Towns*, esp. 112-48. If we consider Daggett to have been, for all practical purposes, an extension of Calico, 1882-1900, then the murder toll rises by four. One particularly gruesome killing, in which a swamper killed a teamster by smashing his head to a pulp with a wagon wheel spoke, resulted in a lynching in 1884. *San Bernardino Times*, December 13,11884; Coroner's inquest, Joseph O. Harris, December 6,1884, San Bernardino County Archives. For Scollard, *The People of the State of California vs. Edward P. Scollard*, 6499 Superior Court, County of San Bernardino (1896), San Bernardino County Archives; Coroner's inquest, Albert P. Roland, May 18,1896, San Bernardino Archives; Baltazar, *Calico*, 47, 54. Also Dix Van Dyke, *Daggett: Life in a Mojave Frontier Town*, edited by Peter Wild (Baltimore: The Johns Hopkins University Press, 1997).

Chapter 6

REMEMBERING CALICO: HISTORICAL MIRAGES

. . . no matter how you look at it or at what time of day, the place is moving and haunting.

Edwin Corle, 1940.

More souls slept in the cemetery than lived in Calico after the lapse of silver and borax mining there. The camp withered, yet it did not completely die. A few steadfast individuals and families always lived there. Some never left. Others did so, and returned. Memories of what had been faded with the passage of time. As they became less distinct, reality gave way to shimmering, sometimes alluring, images that tricked the imagination and beckoned much as desert mirages do. This chapter considers how our memory of Calico took, and retains, its form. Two stories will serve as a prelude for discussion.

The first involved a showing of Kevin Costner's film *Dances With Wolves* in the spring of 1991. In the theatre audience was an 83-year-old, much-crippled woman of the Ho-jak (Winnebago) nation, whose native language was a dialect of Lakota. Born, and reared until she was six years old, in a wigwam, she had then been sent to a Lutheran boarding school in Wisconsin. There she was taught so well that ever afterward she claimed to have forgotten, as she said when referring to her original tongue, "all that Indian talk." She recalled in later years her father's use of a sweat lodge, but only as a form of bathing rather than as an act with spiritual significance. She married "white" and had lived in the white world for more

than three quarters of a century when she saw the film. But part way
through it, as Wind in His Hair was speaking, she straightened her bent
body and said, excitedly, "I know what they are saying. I can understand
them." Education and experience had not so much erased memories as they
had altered or buried them. In doing so, they had rendered parts of reality
indistinct or even invisible, just as the refraction of light on a torrid desert
day produces a mirage that distorts or obscures the actual scene.

The second story resides in an incident in John Nichols' novel *The
Milagro Beanfield War*. Sheriff Bernabé Montoya has appeared at the
United States Forest Service's district office just in time to avert a shootout. Ranger Carl Abeyta, who is in cahoots with a corrupt real estate
developer with plans to destroy the village of Milagro and replace it with a
resort, has lured protagonist Joe Mondragón's milk cow on to national forest
land and impounded it, to break Mondragón's resistance to the development
scheme. Mondragón is trying to retrieve his cow. Abeyta has drawn his
pistol on Joe and ordered him to leave the cow. In turn, four aged Hispanic
friends of Joe comprising the "senile brigade" have arrived in a pickup truck
and waveringly trained their ancient rifles on Carl. Bernabé asks Carl to put
down his weapon. "I do that and they'll shoot me in cold blood," replies
Abeyta. When Bernabé asks the occupants of the pickup whether that is
true, Nichols drily tells us, "the boys all just slightly nodded their heads
yes."[1]

We laugh at the encounter, which ends peacefully, for several reasons.
Of these the most important is that we bring to it culturally shaped
expectations, which stand in the place of memories. These, of the Old West,
refract the contemporary western event that Nichols has related and make
it hilarious. The New Mexican setting, drawn guns, and cow at the action's
center all evoke popular images of the frontier. They are central to several
wonderfully incongruous juxtapositions. There are the substitution of
pickup trucks for horses, and the figure of Joe on foot leading a lone milk
cow instead of a mounted gang attempting to rustle a herd. The weapons
pointed at Carl rest unsteadily in four very old sets of hands. The feebleness
and weak eyesight of the senile brigade make its determination ridiculous.
Comedy arises from the extravagant contrast between what culturally
conditioned expectations, in effect memories, lead us to anticipate, and the
incident related, no less than from Nichols' marvelous use of understatement
in his telling of the story. Cultural predispositions have sharpened, rather
than dulled, our reactions.

The tendencies evident in both of these stories figured in shaping what
later generations recalled of Calico. Those recollections, with the passing

years, came to exaggerate some aspects of the mining center's story and minimize, even disregard, others. The result was the growth of a mythic account, which in time took on a life of its own.

Visiting Calico sixty years after the first silver strikes there and roughly the same number of years before the present, in 1940, a writer captured the essence of a mythic Calico that had already taken form. He had first journeyed there seven years previously, to view the camp by moonlight in connection with a story about a ghost town. Although the place was "not pretty. It's as ugly as sin," he found himself drawn back. The mountains there were, if barren and forbidding, as colorful as the Grand Canyon. The slumbering, nearly vacant camp, sitting deep in a cleft in the range offered no view (the writer exercised artistic license here) of the modern world outside. Buildings still stood in good enough repair to create the illusion of a real frontier mining community, much as a movie set would have. Although one might suppose that the site could offer more to the imagination by moonlight than by day, that was not so. In fact, ". . . no matter when you look at it, or at what time of day, the place is moving and haunting," he observed.

Countless visitors still find it so. Time has ravaged Calico since the words quoted were penned. Picnickers have stripped boards from ruins to use as fuel for their fires. Souvenir hunters have collected all manner of material remains. Weathering has taken its toll. A severe earthquake centered in Yermo shook the area at 7:28 a.m. on May 18, 1997, knocking down some of the ruins. But remarkable sights where the town stood still await the tourist. In the surrounding hills, mine head frames, ore chutes, and ore bins still stand silent guard in the desert sun. It is possible to motor a loop up Odessa and down Occidental Canyons, and drive through Mule Canyon. Concrete foundations define the sites of Marion, and of the Garfield and Waterloo Mills. One can trace the roadbeds of the long-vanished railroads that served the district. One can almost hear echoes of teamsters' shouts as they urge their animals on. Tunnel entrances pockmark the scene. Heaps of tailings are everywhere. Grave markers in the cemetery hint at many a tale. An incomplete and not very faithful reconstruction of the town and a growing catalog of publications project storied images.[2]

Many people were predisposed to embrace these images when Calico won notice. Vague recollections of the frontier as studied in school, notions gained through reading history and fiction, mental pictures formed while listening to radio dramas, and memories of films and later of television programs all lay ready to be tapped. Numerous stereotyped characters were prepared to take stage center when the popular imagination summoned them up. These included the gritty old prospector, the grasping financier, the shady professional gambler, the evil gunfighter, and the fallen but good-hearted prostitute. Waiting also were the hardworking miners and millers, skilled and cursing teamsters, occasional payroll robbers, kindly physicians, courageous defenders of law and order, sweet school mar'ms, and other stock figures. Such people, and others no less familiar, lived, worked, and died in natural settings that varied but were always rugged and memorable. What remains, or has been reconstructed, of Calico seems to provide all of the required elements of the expected scene.

Moreover, Calico's actual experiences provided ample raw material for fashioning an epic account. Such an account could play to all of the predispositions just noted.

On the borax side there were the great twenty-mule teams and their rigs, vivid symbols of an era and an industry. As many probably traveled between Death Valley and around the Calicos to the railroad at Daggett as to Mojave. They were last used at Borate, and teamsters such as John Delameter and Tom Williams continued to live in the area until well past the middle of the twentieth century. There was "Old Dinah," and locomotives numbers 1 and 2, inexplicably named in reverse order the "Marion" and the "Francis," on the railroad joining Borate with Daggett. There was the towering figure of Borax Smith himself, a man whose entrepreneurial abilities placed him in the company of the Rockefellers, Carnegies, and other giants of the time. There was the fact that deep rock mining for borax, which transformed the industry, began in the Calicos. And it was Calico borax that propelled Smith to the preeminent position in his industry, inspired impressive industrial research and development, and was marketed under a still-familiar trademark.

There was similar potential for mythmaking in the story of Calico as a silver producing center. There *was* a cycle of mutual murder among the discoverers of the Burning Moscow Mine. There *was* a narrowly averted gunfight between employees of the Garfield and Occidental groups of mines. There *was* a payroll robbery that ended with a lethal shootout after an Indian tracker guided a posse to the fugitive. The town *did* burn three times. The *Calico Print*, its paper consumed in flames, did publish one final, extra issue on bedsheets after the last, greatest fire in 1887. Dorsey *did* make his appointed rounds with the mail for a year. There *was* a Hyena House, walled with barrel staves. Its owners *really did* greet newcomers with a wheel barrow and the words, "Free bus to the Hyena House." Guests truly *did* have those wretched breakfasts of beans and whisky set before them.

We know that the actual experience of Calico was much more complex than these sets of simple images. The most vivid memories of the district do not entirely erase the tale of borax mining there. However, they typically touch on it briefly, if at all, and tend to understate   its key role and importance in the development of the borax industry. A few colorful incidents usually receive attention, and that is all. In contrast, the story of Calico and silver has been repeated often and richly embellished. In encountering it one meets with claims that place it among the greatest sources of mineral treasure in the frontier West. What's more, Calico provided a stage for as colorful and riveting a set of characters as graced any frontier mining town. The Mechams substituted for Henry T. P. "Old Pancake" Comstock on Mt. Davidson where a great lode was to be named for him. The fictional Diamond Lil stood in for the Black Hills' Calamity Jane. Henry Markham or Robert Waterman were local counterparts—drawn, to be sure, to a much smaller scale—of Leadville's Horace A. W. Tabor and his "Matchless Mine." Lucy Lane might even remind one, if faintly, of Baby Doe Tabor, Horace's wife. Lucy tenaciously rocked out her years (except for the blistering summers) on the porch of her Calico residence, while Baby Doe hung on to the Matchless, as her husband had told her, until she finally froze to death there. Somehow Borax Smith, the only genuine giant on the local scene, seemed to lurk just offstage, or to appear in only a bit part.

Intent played an interesting role in dimming recollections about borax's history in the district, just as it did in the erasure of cultural memories of the Ho-jak elder educated at the Lutheran boarding school. In this case, it was the intent of his associates, and finally of Borax Smith himself. In devising an advertising strategy, they shrewdly embraced the twenty-mule team brand name, after overcoming Smith's initial opposition. But they then set the scene for the teams in Death Valley rather than the Calicos, beginning a geographic identification that continues to the present. Promotion of the Death Valley connection meant effectively forgetting the Calico connection. Or at least minimizing it to the point of near-invisibility.

In 1927, the Pacific Coast Borax Company shifted its mining operations from Death Valley to the immense borate deposits at Kramer, adjacent to what is now the site of Edwards Air Force Base. Had it followed the usual practice of mining firms, it would have dismantled its Death Valley facilities for reuse elsewhere. These were varied and numerous. They included the Death Valley Railroad, built in 1914. It originated on the Ryan branch (serving the Lila C. Mine) of the Tonopah and Tidewater near Death Valley Junction and extended twenty miles to new mines in the Greenwater Range.

There were a small civic center at the junction, and employees' dormitories at Ryan. In the valley itself was the Greenland Ranch, an incongruous gem-like green oasis set in the forbidding desert landscape. The ranch years before had supplied harvesters of cottonball, and twenty-mule rigs. The company did dismantle and relocate mining and milling machinery. Instead of abandoning its other properties in the area, which would surely have left it one more forgotten region pocked with tunnel entrances, scarred with heaps of tailings, and cluttered with decaying ruins, the company chose a different course. Death Valley was to become a tourist mecca and a new source of revenue.

The dormitories at Ryan underwent a transformation into the Death Valley View Hotel. The civic center at Death Valley Junction became the Amargosa Hotel. The Greenland Ranch metamorphosed into the Furnace Creek Ranch, and the company arranged for construction of the Furnace Creek Inn and resort close by. No longer a means of transporting borates, the railroad now had a new mission. It was to carry throngs of tourists to admire the weirdly spectacular and beautiful scenery and to recreate where borax miners had once toiled and sweated. Shrewd managers brought in an old borax wagon train for display on the grounds of the inn. They arranged in 1932 to bring the rusting remains of Old Dinah, as well. These actions reinforced the memories of the association of borax with Death Valley that would have, without them, dimmed. So did the creation of Death Valley National Monument in 1933, with the energetic encouragement of the borax company—under the circumstances a predictable and perhaps inevitable next step. The lengthy (558 episodes) runs on radio and later television of "Death Valley Days," under a variety of titles, merely consummated a process of image making under way since the 1890s.

Although this story is sufficient to explain how Calico's place in the story of borax mining came to be largely forgotten, one further observation can be made. It is fair to guess that, successful as efforts to connect borax in the popular imagination with twenty mule teams and Death Valley were, borax as an industrial mineral simply lacked the glamour of precious metals. It could scarcely rival silver as the focus of memory for Calico, even had there been an intent for it to do so.[3]

Suggestions of reasons for which memories of Calico as a borax center may have been refracted, or faded, almost from consciousness is not the same as explaining why those of its importance as a silver camp have waxed out of all proportion to its actual significance. Even allowance for the raw materials in the district's history, the striking if not spectacular natural scene, and the glamour associated with silver leaves one desiring more. At least three other elements were involved. All related in one way or another to location.

Calico's physical situation, some eighty-five miles from San Bernardino and twice as far from Los Angeles, was a major factor. It was readily accessible by rail to Daggett and by coach from Daggett during its active years. When motor vehicles became common in the twentieth century, it was even more easily reached. Herman Mellen marveled, in 1952, that a journey that had consumed four days on horseback seventy years before now filled only four hours by automobile.[4] Southern California's burgeoning, automobile-loving population found Calico to be within easy reach. What was true in the 1950s of the old United States highway system was even more true with the completion of the interstate highway system during the following decades.

Calico's situation in time was also critically important. It was born, it flourished, and it decayed on the cusp between the nineteenth and the twentieth centuries. Very early it enjoyed railroad and telegraphic ties to the wider world, and telephonic connections by the mid-1890s. Events there could be and were reported within twenty-four hours throughout California. The *Print* gave it an added outlet on a weekly basis. From its origin, it was an outlier of the industrial world. It was never isolated beyond a frontier. The twentieth century, with its technological advances, introduced additional means of bringing Calico and events in Calico, real or imagined, to the attention of an external and growing audience.

Finally, there was its situation in memory. Teamsters John Delameter and Tom Williams, and carpenter Herman Mellen, were far from alone in surviving well into the twentieth century. Walter Alf, Seymour's son, was long a fixture a Daggett. John and Lucy Lane had left in 1899. They moved from one mining camp to another in the desert west after departing. John even purchased Old Dinah for use in freighting between Rhyolite, Nevada, and a nearby mine. They came back in 1916, after an absence of seventeen years. They remained at Calico, except during the scorching summers, until John's death in 1934 and Lucy's in 1967. From the time of their return, they were Calico's unofficial hosts to the world, while they intermittently continued yearly assessment work on the many local silver claims that they had come to control. Lucy's *Calico Memories* records a rapidly growing flow of visitors. Many who came took away vivid impressions. These in time converged with conscious effort—with intention —to publicize Calico as an historic silver mining center. Here was the obverse of the process by which memories of Calico borax dimmed.

In 1920, Lucy fed a film production company that arrived to use Calico as a setting for "Mining Scenes." This turned out to be only the first of many motion pictures filmed locally. "Driving the Golden Spike" followed in 1922. Among those drawn to the area and whom the Lanes hosted was Earl Derr Biggers, author of the "Charlie Chan" mysteries. Biggers used the Stone Front Building in his *The Chinese Parrot*.[5] In 1926, the year of Biggers' visit, Calico received a new form of attention. *Touring Topics*, the magazine of the Automobile Club of Southern California, featured a collection of photographs of the picturesque ruins there. Throughout this period the Lanes continued to entertain tourists. John, while hoping for a revival of local mines, regaled guests with yarns about how modernity had come to Calico and replaced an idealized "wide open, free life of the early mining camps."[6] Aging freighter Delameter at the end of the decade added his "My Forty Years Pulling Freight," also in *Touring Topics*. He was no less gifted at "slinging" than he was at pulling, at one time or another modestly and inaccurately taking credit for naming Calico, and for building most of the huge wagons drawn by twenty-mule teams. His reminiscence was of the same character, enlarging his own importance and further exaggerating memories of silver mining in the district. It also further sped the growth of interest in the old town as a frontier relic that Southern California's intrepid and multiplying motorists ought to visit.[7]

The natural tendencies of selected, romanticized memories to become more expansive, even as they faded, grew stronger as time passed. Occasionally the process received a boost, and an interesting one at that. Philip Johnston rendered Calico's frontier image more vividly in a 1934 popular article. Two years later, in April 1936, members of *E Clampus Vitus* made a pilgrimage to Calico. There these descendants of California's early miners placed a plaque on the front wall of the Lane residence. Appropriately, it was dedicated to "The Forgotten Miner," and it was displayed where virtually everyone who came to the ghost town would see it. Idwall Jones reached an even wider public with "Painted Hills," in *Westways*, not long afterward. In 1940, an article in a major literary magazine, *The Yale Review*, publicized the old camp. Writer Edwin Corle mused that memories of it had by then acquired an aura of "romantic dust."

Most of Corle's remarks were directed to an event that seemed to be filled with contradictions. The event was called "Calico Days," but it took place in Yermo. Although its aim was to celebrate a former mining settlement, it combined elements of a rodeo with those of a carnival. The most important sponsors lived in Barstow, although old Tom Williams of Yermo was a key figure in its inception. It had originated in 1938, a year after the Barstow *Printer-Review* had begun publication of an annual

Special Calico Edition. It was, more than anything else, expressive of small-town boosterism and the desire of people in Barstow to stimulate tourism as a means of combating the depression. By any standard, its connection with history was tenuous. It was a shabby, dusty, disappointing affair. Nevertheless, it attracted each year representatives from the thinning ranks of old-timers. These were ready to swap and share tales both short and tall. And, tawdry as Calico Days were, these events had not dimmed Calico's capacity, wrote Corle, to awaken the imagination. He wondered, then, whether people sixty years hence, in 2000, might react to legends of Calico Days as his own generation did to legends "of the original town today—stories of taking fifty million in silver out of the Calico mountains in a matter of weeks. Or was it eighty million in fifteen years? Nobody seems to be sure." He guessed they would.[8]

The arrival in Yermo in 1934 of Larry and Lucille Coke bears special mention in any discussion of the ways in which Calico came to be remembered. They quickly developed a passionate interest in the site and its history. They began eagerly to explore the Calico Mountains and collect artifacts for a museum, hoping to preserve as much of the record of the past as they could. They added to a treasure trove of mining artifacts an array of other relics, including buried Chinaware, fragments of old store account books, and a vast miscellany illustrating the details of Calico life. They found the old cemetery heavily damaged. Grave robbers and vandals had dug up many of the remains and left a ghastly scattering of bones. Sometimes the Cokes succumbed to an excess of zeal. They repaired the cemetery, and very likely joined with others involved in Calico Days in adding some of the fanciful epitaphs that greet visitors today. They also collected more than three hundred metates and manos used by local Indians to grind seed before European settlers displaced them. They sold their museum in 1939. Their interest, however, did not diminish. In 1941, they published *Calico*, a small, fifty-six page booklet containing a group of colorful anecdotes, many of them of dubious veracity. Long a collector's item, the piece over the following half century influenced much else that was remembered, and written, about Calico.[9]

The next half century brought a growing stream of newspaper travel features, popular magazine articles, and popular historical writing that added to interest in Calico. By the early 1950s, the process of constructing a mythic Calico was essentially complete. Details were added here and there, occasionally a new incident "remembered" or, more accurately, invented. The *Barstow Printer-Review* continued to offer its annual Calico edition. The Cokes from 1950 to 1953 offered a new *Calico Print* as a magazine. Readers had a range of choices when it came to considering what Calico's silver output was. There were published references, all claiming to be authoritative and most actually citing county production, that set it at $13.8 million, something more than $20 million, $26 million, $60 million, $65 million, and a fabulous $86 million. The historical writer for the *San Bernardino Sun-Telegram* was conspicuous in such company for his unswerving regard for accuracy. In reviewing this mass of writing, the interplay of memory of the actual past with the tendencies of old timers to exaggerate, and with the more frankly commercial motives of boosters of tourism and events such as Calico Days, emerge as key themes. That is to say, the growth of the myth was nothing so much as the result of intent.[10]

The final chapter of Calico's history is still being written. In a sense, it began when the Cokes sold their museum. Among those who stopped at the facility after it changed hands was Walter Knott, whose interest earlier visits had kindled. Knott had good reason to feel ties to Calico. Sheriff John King, as we noted earlier, was his uncle. In 1915 he was working in Calico as a carpenter, when World War I sparked a brief rise in silver prices and a short-lived resumption of mining. He returned again after marrying in Pomona and failing at ranching on the Mojave River near Barstow. By 1920 he was gone for good, having moved to Buena Park to enter berry farming. This agricultural venture grew within a generation into one of Southern California's best-known attractions, Knott's Berry Farm. Among its most popular features was Ghost Town, with the Calico Saloon. Knott's recollections of Calico, even of where many of its early buildings had stood, remained vivid. Where memory was insufficient, imagination filled in the gaps.

In 1951 Knott bought the land on which Calico had stood and seventy-five adjacent acres, for $75,000. He pledged to restore the place as an historical and educational site. Work began in 1952. Among other things, safety considerations forced inspection and closure of five thousand feet of shafts and hundreds of hazardous holes. Inspectors examined thirty miles of tunnels. Knott brought on Fred Noller to supervise the work, and artist Paul Van Klieben to design the new buildings from old sketches and photographs. Crews pulled up track, recovered ore cans and cars, cleared sumps, and used aerial photographs as a guide to placement of reconstructed buildings. By 1960, thirty buildings stood along Calico Street. Abutting it was space cleared for automobile parking. Visitors could purchase a booklet, *Calico*, which Knott published in 1952 as a publicity piece. Like the Cokes' earlier pamphlet of the same title, this was largely anecdotal.

Like the reconstruction of the town, it was also none too accurate, although it did reproduce a number of period photographs that captured something of the ambience of old Calico. In 1965, Knott transferred the town site to San Bernardino County, for management as a unit in the county park system. There it remains. The county has cleared much of lower Wall Street Canyon and graded a large parking area there. It has also created a camping area for tent campers and recreational vehicles and developed the site further as an historical attraction. Under the terms of the transfer of title, Knott interests retained the right to operate all commercial concessions in the park. The curator of the Mojave River Valley Museum maintains that Calico is the only county park that earns a profit.[11]

The accuracy of the curator's assertion is far less important than the statement that the reconstructed Calico makes. Visitors to the park encounter reenactors, who represent it as a frontier mining camp that produced a prodigal $86 million in silver. They may learn about Dorsey the mail dog, the Hyena House, the tragic tale of the Burning Moscow. Where there really was a house made of kerosene cans they can view one made of glass bottles cemented together. They do not, however, learn what Calico teaches of the mining West. They capture no sense of its place in the growth of the borax industry, of one of our earliest multinational firms, of Borax Smith as an heroic entrepreneur. They gain no sense of its role as a dependent outlier of an urbanizing, industrializing economy, nor what it showed of technological, economic, and cultural dependence and interdependence. Apart from what they can glean by visiting the Maggie Mine, a schoolhouse, a store or two, Lucy Lane's house, and a make-believe saloon, they acquire only the slenderest grasp of what it was to live and work there. What they experience is a mythic Calico. The myth, like all myths, contains truth. But in this case, not enough. In its selectivity, to serve the varied purposes of its creators, it conceals more than it reveals. That is unfortunate. The reality was far more interesting, and illuminating, than the myth that replaced it.

NOTES

1. John Nichols, *The Milagro Beanfield War* (New York: Ballantine Books, 1974), 269. In the film version, the question is whether the brigade will "shoot . . .[Carl's] nuts off" if he puts down his weapon. The answer is the same.

2. Quotations, Edwin Corle, "CALICO DAYS," *Yale Review*. 30 (Spring, 1940), 549-551.

3. For the railroad, Gordon Chapell, "By Rail to the Rim of Death Valley: Construction of the Death Valley Railroad," *Journal of the West*, 31 (January, 1992), 10-20; for the Furnace Creek Inn, Old Dinah, and the national monument, H[arrison]. P[reston]. Gower, *50 Years in Death Valley: Memories of a Borax Man* (N. P. [San Bernardino?]: Published by the Death Valley '49ers, 1969), 10-11, 26-27, 73, 107-9. The classic promotional piece associating Death Valley and borax, as we saw in Chapter 3, was Spears, *Illustrated Sketches of Death Valley*.

4. Mellen, "Reminiscences," 34, 363-64.

5. Earl Derr Biggers, *The Chinese Parrot* (Indianapolis: The Bobbs-Merrill Company, 1926); Lane, *Memories*, 55, 56.

6. Anonymous, "Where Calico Once Thrived," *Touring Topics*, 18 (May, 1926), 30-34; quotation, Lane, *Memories*, 56.

7. John A. Delameter, "My Forty Years," 24-29. For comments on Delameter, see Harold O. Weight, *Twenty Mule Days*, 1-14.

8. Philip Johnston, "Silver & Calico," *Westways*, 26 (November, 1934), 18-19, 38-39; Lane, *Memories*, 53-70; Idwall Jones, "Painted Hills," *Westways*, 31 (August, 1939), 20-21; Corle, "Calico Days," 557-58.

9. Larry and Lucille Coke, *Calico* (Barstow: *Barstow Printer-Review*, 1941).

10. There is need to cite only a few illustrative titles here. For examples, John W. Garner, "Calico Cemetery," *The Desert Magazine*, 5 (February, 1942), 40; F. Conrad, "The Singing Calico Hills," *Pacific Pathways*, 2 (April, 1947), 17-20; Harold O. Weight, "Gray Ghosts of Calico," *Westways*, 41 (March, 1949), 14-15; Anonymous [Larry and Lucille Coke], "Calico School District," "Calico's Silver Circle," "Early Days in Odessa Canyon," *Calico Print*, 6 (July, 1950), 4, 7 (January, 1951), 4, 5; Anonymous [Remi Nadeau], "Old Calico—Model Ghost Town," *Fortnight*, 13 (November, 1952), 29-30, reprinted in Remi Nadeau, *Ghost Towns of California* (Los Angeles: *Fortnight Magazine*, 1955), 59-61. Also Lucille Coke, "Tales of Old Calico: The Jinx of the Burning Moscow," Coke, ". . . The King Claim, Calico's 'Mother Lode,'"; Coke, ". . . When Johnny and Fiddlin: Bob Raced the Pale Rider," all *Calico Print*, 7 (January, 1951), 1, 7 and 1-7; 6(November, 1950), 1-2; and L. Burr Belden, "Calico Booms as County's Biggest Silver Camp," *San Bernardino Sun-Telegram*, November 2,1952; "Mechams Tell of Calico Silver Camp Discovery," *San Bernardino Sun-Telegram*, October 26,1952; "Calico Booms in 1800s, Fades as Silver Declines," *San Bernardino Sun-Telegram*, March 6,1960, are among Belden's dozens of feature stories.

For the lower estimates of silver output, Emile Huguenin Cloudman and others, *Fifteenth Report of the State Mineralogist* (Sacramento, 1919), 823-25; and Lloyd L. Root, "Chapter of Report XXII of the State Mineralogist," *Mining in California* (San Francisco, 1926), 384. Larry and Lucille Coke, *Calico*, claimed a production of "over sixty million dollars," p. 20, and an output of $65 million, p. 7; Muriel Wolle, *The Bonanza Trail: Ghost Towns and Mining Camps of the West* (Bloomington, 1953), 141-47, probably followed the Cokes in claiming $65 million, as did Mary R. Hill, "Silver," *Mineral Information Service*, 16 (June, 1963), 7. For $86 million, Anonymous [Knott], *Calico* and W. Storrs Lee, *The Great California Deserts* (New York, 1963), 159. J. T. Weakely, who for a time owned both the Silver King and the Waterloo groups of mines and their records writes that through the 1920s they had yielded $12 million and $9 million respectively. J. T. Weakely, personal letter to the author, May 9,1958.

11. Some of this history is recounted in Warren Dean Starr, "History of the Settlement and Development of Calico, California, to 1900 (unpublished master's thesis, Washington State University, 1963), 99-107; author's interview with Bill Tomlinson, Curator, Mojave River Valley Museum, July 29,1997, by telephone to Barstow, California. Published references include Harold O. Weight, "Man Who Bought A Ghost Town," *Desert Magazine*, 16 (July, 1953),   14-18.   Archival sources pertaining to town site land transfers follow. **DEED**, Walter, Cordelia, and Russell Knott, and Knott's Berry Farm **TO** Calico Land and Improvement Corporation. Filing Date, February 27,1964. *Document No. 639, Official Records Book 6097*, Recorder, County of San Bernardino, 530. **DEED**, Walter, Cordelia, and Russell Knott, and Knott's Berry Farm **TO** Calico Corners, Inc. Filing Date, February 27,1964. *Document No.* 640, *Official Records Book 6097*, Recorder, County of San Bernardino, 532. **ASSIGNMENT OF LEASE**, Walter, Cordelia, and Russell Knott, and Knotts Berry Farm **TO** Calico Land and Improvement Corporation. Filing Date, May 18,1964, *Document No.* 494, *Official Records Book 6151*, Recorder, County of San Bernardino, 418. **DEED**, Walter, Cordelia, and Russell H. Knott, and Knotts Berry Farm **TO** County of San Bernardino. Filing Date, October 30,1964. *Document No.* 874, *Official Records Book 6263*, Recorder, County of San Bernardino, 418. **DEED**, Walter, Cordelia, and Russell H. and Mildred N. Knott, and Knotts Berry Farm **TO** County of San Bernardino. Filing Date, November 3,1965. *Document No.* 394, *Official Records Book 6505*, Recorder, County of San Bernardino, 974. These are all cited in the *INDEX TO OFFICIAL RECORDS, 1964-1965*, San Bernardino County Archives. Finally, "APPLICATION FOR THE REGISTRATION OF CALICO AS A CALIFORNIA HISTORICAL LANDMARK," July 1,1962 (unpublished manuscript), San Bernardino County Archives offers information pertinent to its subject.

Appendix

By-laws of the Calico Mining District

SEC.   I. Calico Mining District shall be bounded as follows: Commence at a point about two and a half miles west of the Calico Well (better known as the little red butte),[1] run thence ten miles north, thence ten miles east, thence ten miles south, thence ten miles west to the point of beginning.

SEC.   II. The name of the District shall be Calico.

SEC.   III. This District shall have one officer, viz: A Recorder, whose office shall be in Calico.

SEC.   IV. The Recorder shall hold his office for one year, beginning the 1st day of June and ending the last day of May, provided, his successor has been previously elected; otherwise he shall hold his office until the election of a successor.

SEC.   V. It shall be the duty of the Recorder to keep a record-book for the purpose of recording claims and affidavits of assessment work.[2]

SEC.   VI. The Recorder shall receive one dollar for recording claims, fifty cents for recording affidavits, and twenty-five cents for furnishing certificates.

SEC.   VII. It shall be the duty of the Recorder to post notices of election, in three public places, ten days before the expiration of his term.

SEC.   VIII. At the request of five miners, the Recorder shall call a miners' meeting. The notice of the meeting shall set forth the object for which it is called.

SEC.   IX. Provided the limits of the district are to be changed or the By-laws amended, the Recorder shall give notice of such changes or amendments twenty days beforehand by posing notices in three public places in the district.

SEC.   X. It shall be the duty of the Recorder to turn over to his successor all books and papers pertaining to the archives of the district.

SEC.   XI. The width of lode claims shall be three hundred feet on each side of the center of a vein or crevice.[3]

SEC. XII. The discoverer of a lode shall, within ninety days from the date of discovery, record his claim in the office of the Recorder of this district, which record shall contain: 1st, the name of the lode [assigned by the discoverer]; 2nd, the name of the locator; 3rd, the date of the locations; 4th, the number of feet in length claimed on each side of the discovery shaft; 5th, the general course of the lode as near as may be.

SEC. XIII. Any location certificate of a lode claim which shall not contain the name of the lode, the name of the locator, the date of location, the number of lineal feet claimed on each side of the discovery shaft, the general course of the lode, and such description as shall identify the claim with reasonable certainty, shall be void.

SEC. XIV. Before filing such location certificate the discoverer shall locate his claim by first sinking a discovery shaft upon the lode, to the depth of at least ten feet from the lowest part of the rim of such shaft at the surface, or deeper if necessary to show a well-defined crevice. Second, by posting at the point of discovery or [on] the surface, a conspicuous notice containing the name of the lode, the name of the locator, and the date of discovery. Third, by marking the surface boundaries of the claim.

SEC. XV. Such surface boundaries shall be marked by nine substantial posts or monuments, three on each end and three on a line running through the center.

SEC. XVI. Any open cut, cross-cut or tunnel, which shall cut a lode at the depth of ten feet below the surface, shall hold such lode the same as if a discovery shaft were sunk thereon; or an adit [horizontal mine entrance] at least ten feet along the lode, from the point where the lode may be in any manner discovered, shall be equivalent to a discovery shaft.

SEC. XVII. The discoverer shall have sixty days from the time of discovering a ledge or lode to do the necessary work on his claim.

SEC. XVIII. If at any time the locator of any mining claim heretofore or hereafter located, or his assigns, shall apprehend that his original certificate was defective, erroneous, or that the requirements of the law had not been complied with before filing; or shall be desirous of changing his surface boundaries; or of taking in any part of an overlapping claim which has been abandoned, such locator or his assigns may file an additional certificate; provided that such re-location does not interfere with the existing rights of others at the time of such re-location; and the record thereof shall preclude the claimants from proving such title or titles as he or they may have held under previous location.

SEC. XIX. The re-location of abandoned lode claims shall be by sinking a new discovery shaft, fix[ing] new boundaries in the same manner as if it were the new location of a new claim; or the re-locator may sink the discovery shaft ten feet deeper than it was at the time of abandonment, and erect new or adopt the old boundaries, renewing the monuments if removed or destroyed. In either case, a new location stake or monument shall be erected. In any case, whether the whole or part of an abandoned claim is taken, the location certificate may state that the whole or any part of the new location is located as abandoned property.

SEC. XX. No location certificate shall claim more than one location, whether the location be made by one or several locators; and if it purport to claim more than one location, it shall be absolutely void, except as to the first location therein described. And if they are described together, or so that it cannot be told which location is described, the certificate shall be void as to all.

SEC. XXI. Within thirty days after performing the assessment work on a claim the person on whose behalf such outlay was made, or some person for him, shall make and record an affidavit in substance as follows:

STATE OF CALIFORNIA
COUNTY OF SAN BERNARDINO

Before me, the subscriber, personally appeared _____,
who being duly sworn said that at least _____ Dollars worth of work or
improvements were performed upon (here describe claim or part or claim), situate[d] in
Calico Mining District, County of San Bernardino, State of California. Such expenditure
was made by or at the expense of _____, owners of said
claim.

(Signature)

And such signature shall be prima facie evidence of the performance of such
labor.

SEC. XXII. The By-laws shall take effect on the tenth day of June, 1882.

NOTES

1. The well was located at the edge of Calico Dry Lake, about a mile south of the point
at which Wall Street Canyon debauches onto the desert floor. The butte in question stands
almost in the middle of Section 30 of Township 20 North (of the San Bernardino
Baseline), Range 1 East (of the San Bernardino Meridian), about two and one-half miles
west of the old well site.

2. Unless he purchased a mining property outright from the federal government, or
from a prior operator who held it in fee simple and had obtained from the government a
patent of ownership for it, a claim holder enjoyed only a usufructory right. This right was
forfeit, unless the holder annually filed an affidavit attesting to the fact that either he
himself or someone in his employ had performed at least $100 worth of work or made at
least $100 in improvements on the claim during the preceding year. This labor, because
it was levied or assessed of claim holders, was known as assessment work.

3. The federal mining statute of 1872 prescribed means for filing for claims, the
assessment work to be performed in order to retain rights to a claim, the maximum size
(twenty acres) and boundaries (1,500 feet along a vein and three hundred feet on either
side), notice requirements, and so on. See *United States Code*, 1958 Edition, 6
(Washington, 1959), 4,484-4,487.

SELECT BIBLIOGRAPHY

PRIMARY SOURCES

Public or Official Documents

Annual Reports of the California State Mineralogist [titles vary; various authors], 1884-1930. Sacramento: State of California, 1884-1930.

Bailey, Gilbert E., *Register of Mines and Minerals [San Bernardino County, California]*. Sacramento: State of California, 1902.

_____, *The Saline Deposits of California*. Sacramento: State of California, 1902.

Bowen, Oliver E., Jr., *Mines and Mineral Deposits of Barstow Quadrangle San Bernardino County, California*. San Francisco: N.P., 1954.

Campbell, Marius R., *Borax Deposits of Death Valley and Mojave Desert*. Washington: Government Printing Office, 1902.

Erwin, Homer D., and Dion L. Garner, "Notes on the Geology of a Portion of the Calico Mountains, San Bernardino County, California," *California Journal of Mines and Geology* 36 (July, 1940), 193-304.

Gates, Paul Wallace, *History of Public Land Law Development*. Washington: Government Printing Office, 1968.

Hill, James M., *The Mining Districts of the Western United States*. Washington: Government Printing Office, 1912.

Hill, Mary R., "Silver," *Mineral Information Service*, State of California, Division of Mines and Geology, 16 (June, 1963), 1-8.

Mineral Resources of the United States [authors, editors vary], *1891-1915* [for borax]. Washington, D.C.: Government Printing Office, 1893-1917.

Murdoch, Joseph, and Robert W. Webb, *Minerals of California*. San Francisco: State of California, 1948.

Ricketts, A. H., *American Mining Law, With Forms and Precedents*. 4th Ed. Sacramento: State of California, 1948.

Stipp, Henry E., "Borax," *Mineral Facts and Problems*. 1960 Edition. Washington: Government Printing Office, 1960.

Thompson, David Grosh, *Routes to Desert Watering Places in the Mohave Desert Region, California.* Washington: Government Printing Office, 1921.

_____, *The Mohave Desert Region, California: Geographic, Geologic, and Hydrologic Reconnaissance.* Washington: Government Printing Office, 1929.

_____, *The Old Government Road Across the Mohave Desert to Needles.* San Bernardino: State Emergency Relief Administration, 1939.

Tucker, W. B., and R. J. Sampson, "Current Mining Activity in Southern California," *California Journal of Mines and Geology*, 36 (January, 1940), 59-60.

_____, "Economic Mineral Deposits of the Newberry and Ord Mountains, San Bernardino County," *California Journal of Mines and Geology*, 36 (July, 1940), 241-244.

United States, Bureau of the Census, *Historical Statistics of the United States: Colonial Times to 1957.* Washington: Government Printing Office, 1960.

_____, Bureau of Statistics, *Statistical Abstract of the United States, 1900.* Washington: Government Printing Office, 1901.

_____, *Census Office, Compendium of the Eleventh Census: 1890. Part I. — Population.* Washington: Government Printing Office, 1892. I.

_____, *Eleventh Census of the United States: 1890.* Washington: Government Printing Office, 1892. VII.

_____, *Twelfth Census of the United States. Taken in the Year 1900. Population, Part I.* Washington: Government Printing Office, 1901. I.

United States Code, 1958, 6. Washington: Government Printing Office, 1958: 5,485-5,487. Title 30, Chapter 2, Sections 22-29.

_____, House of Representatives, 56 Congress, 2 Session, *Document No.* 239, "Report of the Director of the Mint Upon the Production of Precious Metals in the United States During the Calendar Year 1899."

_____, 48 Cong., 1 Sess.—52 Cong., 2 Sess., *Executive Document* Nos. [vary from year to year], "Precious Metals . . . 1883—1892."

_____, *Report No.* 1, "Proposed Revision of the Tariff [1897]."

_____, 55 Cong., 1 Sess., *Senate Document No.* 188, "Comparison of the Tariff Act of August 28,1894 . . . [with that of 1897]."

_____, 53 Cong., 1 Sess., *Senate Report No.* 707, "Bulletin No. 61, Part I. Committee on Finance, United States Senate, The Customs Law of 1894."

_____, "Bulletin No. 61, Part II. . . . Comparison of the Text of the Tariff Laws of 1890 and 1894."

_____, 53 Cong., 1 Sess., *Senate Report No.* 708. "Bulletin 62, Part I. Committee on Finance, United States Senate. Table of Average Ad Valorem Rates . . . ."

Verplanck, William E., "History of Borax Production in the United States," *California Journal of Mines and Geology*, 52 (July, 1956), 273-291.

Weber, Harold F., Jr., "Silver Deposits of the Calico District, Part II," *Mineral Information Service*, California Division of Mines and Geology, 20 (January, 1967), 3-7.

_____, "Silver Deposits of the Calico Mining District, Part III," *Mineral Information Service*, 20(February, 1967), 11-15.

_____, "Silver Mining in Old Calico," *Mineral Information Service*, 19 (May, 1966), 71-80.

Wright, Lauren A., and Bennie W. Troxel, "Geologic Guide No. 1: Western Mojave Desert and Death Valley Region," *Geology of Southern California*. San Francisco:

State of California, 1954.

____, Richard M. Stewart, Thomas E. Gay, Jr., and George C. Hazenbush, "Mines and Mineral Deposits of San Bernardino County, California," *California Journal of Mines and Geology*, 49 (January-April, 1953), 123-133, 220-225, and *passim*.

Books and Pamphlets

Borax Producers of the Pacific Coast, *Borax Products of the Pacific Coast: Facts and Figures Regarding Borax*. N. P.: N. P., September 1, 1893.

Gerstley, James, *Borax Years: Some Recollections, 1933-1961. The Story of Pacific Coast Borax Company and United States Borax & Chemical Corporation*. Los Angeles: United States Borax Company, 1979.

Gower, H[arrison]. P[reston]., *50 Years in Death Valley—Memoirs of a Borax Man*. N. P. [San Bernardino?]: Death Valley 49ers, 1969.

Lane, Lucy Bell, *Calico Memories of . . . .* Edited by Alan Baltazar. Barstow: Alan Baltazar, 1993.

The Mineral Industry, Its Statistics, Technology, and Trade [various editors; for borax]. New York: The Scientific Publishing Company, 1894-1902.

Polk, R. L., *California State Gazetteer and Business Directory, 1888*. San Francisco: R. L. Polk & Company, 1888.

Spears, John Randolph., *Illustrated Sketches of Death Valley and Other Borax Deserts of the Pacific Coast*. Chicago: Rand McNally Company, 1892.

Van Dyke, Dix, *Daggett: Life in a Mojave Frontier Town*. Edited by Peter Wild. Baltimore: The Johns Hopkins University Press, 1997.

Walker, Charles E., John Flagg, and W. R. McIntosh, *McIntosh, Flagg & Walker's San Bernardino City and County Directory [1889]*. San Bernardino, California: Flagg & Walker, Printers & Binders, 1889.

Newspapers and Periodicals

"Borax," *Scientific American*, 71 (July, 1894), 60-63.

"Borax—Old and New Methods of Production," *Scientific American*, 82 (May 26, 1906), 326.

"Calico District," *Mining and Scientific Press*, 50 (March 14,1885), 173, 180.

Calico Print, July 8,1882-September 5,1887.

"Calico Print, September 20," *Mining and Scientific Press*, 51 (September 20,1885), 216.

"[Various titles from *Calico Print*]," *Mining and Scientific Press*, 45 (July 1,1882) to 54 (March 19,1887).

"CALIFORNIA," and "General," *Mining and Scientific Press*, 48 (January 19,1884), 41, 36.

Delameter, John A., "Calico," *Touring Topics*, 20 (October, 1928), 25-26.

____, "El Oso Viejo," *Touring Topics*, 22 (August, 1930), 18-22.

____, "My 40 Years Pulling Freight," *Touring Topics*, 22 (August, 1930), 24-29.

Foshag, William F., "Calico Hills, San Bernardino Co., California," *The American Mineralogist*, 7 (January, 1922), 208-209.

"General," *Mining and Scientific Press* 45 (July 1, December 30,1882), 2, 421.

"General," *Mining and Scientific Press*, 46 (February 17, March 17, May 10, June 9, all 1883), 109, 181, 341, 389.

"General," *Mining and Scientific Press*, 48 (January 19,1884), 36.

"General," *Mining and Scientific Press*, 49 (August 2,1884), 72.

"John Doe Passes Away," *San Francisco Examiner*, January 22,1894.

"July 1,1882—From the Los Angeles Commercial," *Mining and Scientific Press*, 45 (July 1,1882), 2.

Keyes, Charles R., "Borax Deposits of the United States," *Transactions of the American Institute of Mining Engineers*, 40 (1910), 674-710.

Lindgren, Waldemar, "The Silver Mines at Calico, California," *Transactions of the American Institute of Mining Engineers*, 15 (May, 1886-February, 1887), 717-734.

Los Angeles Times, 1882-1907.

Mellen, Herman F., "The Chinese of Calico," *Calico Print*, 7 (November, 1951), 7.

_____, "Reminiscences of Old Calico," *The Historical Society of Southern California Quarterly*, 34 (June, 1952), 107-124; (September, 1952), 243-260; (December, 1952), 347-364.

_____, "We Called Them Cousin Jacks," *Calico Print*, 6 (December, 1950), 2.

Palmer, Leroy A., "The Calico District, California," *Mining and Scientific Press*, 116 (June, 1918), 755-758.

"San Bernardino," *Mining and Scientific Press*, 54 (March 19,1887), 192.

San Bernardino Index, January-December, 1886.

San Bernardino Sun-Telegram, 1938-1958.

San Bernardino Weekly Times, 1883-1890.

San Francisco Bulletin, January 22,1894.

San Francisco Chronicle, 1882-1907.

Storms, W. H., "The Mines of the Calico District, California," *The Engineering and Mining Journal*, 49 (April 5,1890), 382-383.

Willey, Ray Allen, "Borax Mining in California," *The Engineering and Mining Journal*, 57 (October 6,1906), 633-634.

Archival Sources

Articles of Incorporation, firms incorporated in San Bernardino County, 1882-1907. San Bernardino County Archives.

Assignments of Leases, Records of Deeds, Calico Townsite, *Official Records Books 6151, 6097, 6263, 6505*. Recorder, County of San Bernardino.

Burial and Removal Permits, Calico Cemetery. San Bernardino County Archives.

Cahill, William Washington, "NOTES ON OPERATIONS AT OLD BORATE AS RECALLED BY W. W. CAHILL WHO WENT TO WORK THERE IN 1892." Unpublished manuscript, from H. P. Gower, United States Borax & Chemical Corporation, March 28,1958.

___, "HALF A CENTURY WITH THE PACIFIC COAST BORAX COMPANY AND SUBSIDIARY COMPANIES." Undated manuscript in Ruth C. Woodman   Papers, Department of Special Collections, Library, University of Oregon.

Charge account ledger from a general store in Calico. Lent by Lucille Coke, March, 1956.

Coroner's Inquests, San Bernardino County Archives, 1881-1907.

Doe v. Waterloo Min. Co. (Nos. 160, 161, 2 cases). Circuit Court, S. D. California. 43 *Federal Reports*, 219-223 (August 8,1890).

Doe v. Waterloo Min. Co. (No. 183). Circuit Court, S.D. California. 54 *Federal Reports*, 935-951(March 27,1893).

Doe v. Waterloo Min. Co., SAME v. SAME (Nos. 160, 161), Circuit Court, S. D. California, 55 *Federal Reports*, 11-15 (April 3,1893).

Doe v. Waterloo Min. Co. (No. 183). Circuit Court, S.D. California. 60 *Federal Reports*, 643 (March 22,1894).

Drummond, T. R., "Report on the Property of the Zenda Gold Mining Company, San Bernardino Co., California." Unpublished geological survey of the Zenda group of mines at Calico, lent to the author by J. T. Weakley, Los Angeles. Undated.

Great Register of Voters, Calico Precinct, 1882-1890. San Bernardino County Archives.

Haenzel, Arda M., "APPLICATION FOR REGISTRATION OF CALICO AS A CALIFORNIA HISTORICAL LANDMARK." July 1,1962. San Bernardino County Archives.

Hardy, William S., William L. Miller, and S[tewart]. W. Fulton [?], "Report of Road Commissioners on Public Road near Calico. Unpublished manuscript filed December 1, 1888. San Bernardino County Archives.

Hyde, Leslie Daggett, "John Daggett," D . A. R . Records of the Families of California Pioneers, 19. N.P., N.D. Pp. 60-61.

"Index to Mines. San Bernardino County," volumes I-III. Bound manuscript volumes identifying by name, name of claimant, date of location, all mining claims located in San Bernardino from 1855 onward. San Bernardino County Archives.

Lane, Lucy Bell, *Calico Memories of . . . .* Edited by Alan F. Baltazar. Barstow: Alan Baltazar, 1993.

The People of the State of California, Plaintiffs, vs. Jim Tye, Defendant. Calico Justice Court. January 24,1889. San Bernardino County Archives.

"Records of Silver King Mining Company, Limited. Folder No. 26328," Register of Companies Office, Bush House, London. Available at Bancroft Library, University of California, Berkeley, Film Z GL Reel 96, pt. 3.

Records of the Superior Court of San Bernardino County, San Bernardino County Archives, 1882-1895.

San Bernardino County Supervisors, *Records Books*, C, 384-; D; E; F; G; H; I; -J, 282 (October 4,1882 to January 4,1899). San Bernardino County Archives.

Snell, Charles W., *A Brief History of the Borax Industry of the Pacific Coast, 1864-1914.* Unpublished manuscript, National Park Service, Western Region, San Francisco, January 13,1965.

United States Bureau of Mines, San Francisco, "Mint Records Calico," copied October, 1965. "*Confidential*." Manuscript in possession of the author.

United States Treasury Department, "Report of the Director of the Mint: Precious Metals," October, 1965. "*Confidential*." Manuscript in possession of the author.

Waterloo Min. Co. v. Doe et al. (No. 120), Circuit Court, S.D. California, 56 *Federal Reports*, 685-690 (April 18,1893).

Weber, Harold F., "Bibliography of the Calico silver district and vicinity, San Bernardino County, California." Undated, attached to personal letter to the author, November 30, 1966.

Weeks, F.B., "*Bismarck Mine*, Calico Mining District, San Bernardino Co., California." Unpublished, undated geological survey of the Bismarck group of mines at Calico, lent to the author by J. T. Weakely, Los Angeles.

Williams, Robert G., Compiler, "Calico Cemetery." Unpublished alphabetical listing of grave sites in Calico cemetery, October, 1986. San Bernardino County Archives. Fuller annotations in version in San Bernardino County Library Reference Room.

Woodman, Ruth C., Papers. Department of Special Collections, Library, University of Oregon.

SECONDARY SOURCES

Books and Pamphlets

Abbott, Carl, *Boosters and Businessmen: Popular Economic Thought and Urban Growth in the Antebellum Middle West.* Westport, Connecticut: Greenwood Press, 1981.

Anonymous, *Calico.* Ghost Town, California: Knott's Berry Farm, 1952.

_____, *History of San Bernardino County, California, With Illustrations Descriptive of Its Scenery, Farms, Residences, Public Buildings, Factories, Hotels, Business Houses, Schools, Churches, Etc.* San Francisco: Wallace W. Elliot & Co., Publishers, 1883.

_____, *Romantic Heritage of the Mojave River. A Saga of Transportation and Desert Frontiers.* Barstow: General Telephone Company, 1961.

_____, [Woodman, Ruth, and Ann Rosener], *The Story of the Pacific Coast Borax Company: Division of Borax Consolidated, Limited.* N. P.: Borax Consolidated Limited, 1951.

_____, "Waterman, Robert W.," *The National Cyclopedia of American Biography.* Clifton, New Jersery: J. T. White, 1902.

Atherton, Lewis, *Main Street on the Middle Border.* Bloomington: Indiana University Press, 1954.

Billington, Ray Allen, *America's Frontier Heritage.* New York: Holt, Rinehart & Winston, 1966.

Boorstin, Daniel, *The Americans: The National Experience.* New York: Vintage Books, 1965.

Butler, Anne M., *Daughters of Joy, Sisters of Misery: Prostitutes in the American West, 1865-90.* Urbana: University of Illinois Press, 1985.

Chalfant, W. A., *Death Valley: The Facts.* Palo Alto: Stanford University Press, 1930.

Coke, Larry, and Lucille Coke, *Calico.* Barstow: *Barstow Printer-Review*, 1941.

Douglas, Paul Howard, *Real Wages in the United States, 1860-1914.* Boston: Houghton Mifflin Company, 1934.

Doyle, Don Harrison, *The Social Order of a Frontier Community: Jacksonville, Illinois, 1825-70.* Urbana: University of Illinois Press, 1978.

Dykstra, Robert R., *The Cattle Towns: A Social History of the Kansas Cattle Trading Centers of Abilene, Ellsworth, Wichita, Dodge City and Caldwell, 1867-1885.* New York: Atheneum, 1970.

Fels, Rendigs. *American Business Cycles, 1865-1897.* Chapel Hill: The University of North Carolina Press, 1959.

Frisch, Michael, *Town into City.* Cambridge: Harvard University Press, 1972.

Friedman, Milton, and Anna Jacobson Schwartz, *A Monetary History of the United States, 1867-1960.* Princeton: Princeton University Press, 1963.

Griffith, Sally Foreman, *Home Town News: William Allen White & the Emporia Gazette.* New York: Oxford University Press, 1989.

Hafen, LeRoy, and Ann W. Hafen, *Old Spanish Trail: Santa Fe to Los Angeles.* Lincoln: University of Nebraska Press, 1982.

Hildebrand, George Herbert, *Borax Pioneer: Francis Marion Smith.* San Diego: Howell-North Books, 1982.

Hoffman, Charles, *The Depression of the 1890s—An Economic History.* Westport,

Connecticut: Greenwood Press, 1970.

Ingersoll, Luther A., *Ingersoll's Century Annals of San Bernardino County*. Los Angeles: Luther A. Ingersoll, 1904.

Lee, W. Storrs, *The Great California Deserts*. New York: G. P. Putnam's Sons, 1963.

Lord, Eliot, *Comstock Mines and Miners*. A Reprint of the 1883 Edition with Introduction by David F. Myrick. Berkeley: Howell-North Books, 1959.

McPhee, John, *Basin and Range*. New York: Farrar Straus and Giroux [The Noonday Press], 1980.

Myers, Sandra L., *Westering Women and the Frontier Experience 1800-1915*. Albuquerque: University of New Mexico Press, 1982.

Myrick, David F., *Railroads of Nevada and Eastern California: II, The Southern Roads*. Berkeley: Howell-North Books, 1963.

Nadeau, Remi, *Ghost Towns and Mining Camps of California*. Los Angeles: The Ward Ritchie Press, 1965.

_____, *Ghost Towns of California*. Los Angeles: Fortnight Magazine, 1955.

Ong, Fr. Walter J., *Orality and Literacy: The Technologizing of the Word*. New York: Methuen, 1982.

Paul, Rodman W., *California Gold: The Beginning of Mining in the Far West*. Cambridge: Harvard University Press, 1967.

_____, *The Far West and the Great Plains in Transition, 1859-1900*. New York: Harper & Row Publishers, 1988.

_____, *Mining Frontiers of the Far West, 1848-1880*. New York: Holt, Rinehart and Winston, 1963.

Rees, Albert, *Real Wages in Manufacturing, 1890-1914*. Princeton: Princeton University Press, 1961.

Scherer, James B., *The Lion of the Vigilantes: William T. Coleman and the Life of Old San Francisco*. Indianapolis: The Bobbs-Merrill Company, 1939.

Shinn, Charles Howard, *Land Laws of Mining Districts*. Baltimore: The Johns Hopkins University Press, 1884.

Spence, Clark, *British Investments and the American Mining Frontier, 1860-1901*. Moscow: University of Idaho Press, 1995.

Travis, Norman J., and E. J. Cocks, *The Tincal Trail: A History of Borax*. London: Harrap Limited, 1984.

_____, and Carl L. Randolph, *United States Borax and Chemical Corporation: The First Hundred Years*. New York: The Newcomen Society in North America, 1973.

United States Borax and Chemical Corporation, *The Story of Borax*. Glendale: United States Borax & Chemical Corporation, 1979.

Vredenburgh, Larry M., Gary L. Shumway, and Russel D. Hartill, *Desert Fever: An Overview of Mining in the California Desert*. Canoga Park: Living West Press, 1981.

Weight, Harold O., *Twenty Mule Team Days in Death Valley*. Twenty Nine Palms: The Calico Press, 1955.

White, Richard, *"It's Your Misfortune and None of My Own": A New History of the American West*. Norman: University of Oklahoma Press, 1991.

Wiebe, Robert, *The Search for Order, 1877-1920*. New York: Hill and Wang, 1967.

Williams, David, *The Georgia Gold Rush: Twenty-Niners, Cherokees, and Gold Fever*. Columbia: University of South Carolina Press, 1993.

Wolle, Muriel Sibel, *The Bonanza Trail: Ghost Towns and Mining Camps of the West*. Bloomington: Indiana University Press, 1953.

Newspapers and Periodicals

Barstow Printer-Review, May 12, 1938; May 11,1939; January 25,1940; May 9,1940; March 26,1953.

Belden, L. Burr, "Calico Booms as County's Biggest Silver Camp," *San Bernardino Sun-Telegram*, November 2,1952.

_____, "Calico Booms in 1800s, Fades as Silver Declines," *San Bernardino Sun-Telegram*, March 6,1960.

_____, "Mechams Tell of Calico Silver Camp Discovery" *San Bernardino Sun-Telegram*, October 26,1952.

"Calico," *Death Valley Days*, KTTV, Los Angeles, California, December 6,1961 [script].

Chapell, Gordon, "By Rail to the Rim of Death Valley: Construction of the Death Valley Railroad," *Journal of the West*, 31 (January, 1992), 10-20.

[Coke, Lucille], "Calico School District," *Calico Print*, 6 (July, 1950), 4.

[Coke, Lucille], "Calico's Silver Circle," *Calico Print*, 7 (January, 1951), 4.

[Coke, Lucille], "Early Days in Odessa Canyon," *Calico Print*, 7 (January, 1951), 5.

Coke, Lucille, "Tales of Old Calico: The Jinx of the Burning Moscow," *Calico Print*, 7 (January, 1951), 1, 7.

_____, "Tales of Old Calico: The King Claim, Calico's 'Mother Lode,'" *Calico Print*, 7 (January, 1951), 1-7.

_____, "Tales of Old Calico: When Johnny and Fiddlin' Bob Raced the Pale Rider," *Calico Print*, 6 (November, 1950), 1-2.

Conrad, "The Singing Calico Hills," *Pacific Pathways*, 2 (April, 1947), 17-20.

Corle, Edwin, "Calico Days," *Yale Review*, 30 (Spring, 1940), 549-559.

Garner, John W., "Calico Cemetery," *The Desert Magazine*, 5 (February, 1941), 40.

Hill, Jim Dan, "The Early Mining Camp in American Life," *The Pacific Historical Review*, 1 (August, 1832), 295-311.

Johnston, Philip, "Silver & Calico," *Westways*, 26 (November, 1934), 18-19, 38-39.

Jones, Idwall, "Painted Hills," *Westways*, 31 (August, 1939), 20-21.

Keagle, Cora P., "Buckboard Days in Borate," *Desert Magazine*, 2 (September, 1939), 25-27.

_____, "Odessa," *Desert Magazine*, 2 (May, 1938), 14-19.

McKay, J., "Old Calico," *Desert Magazine*, 2 (May, 1939), 15-16.

[Nadeau, Remi], "Old Calico-Model Ghost Town," *Fortnight*, 13 (November, 1952), 29-30.

Weber, Harold F., "Economic Geology of the Calico District, California." Preprint of paper presented to Society of Mining Engineers, Las Vegas, Nevada, September 6-8,1967.

Weight, Harold O., "Grey Ghosts of Calico," *Westways*, 41 (March, 1949), 14-15.

_____, "Man Who Bought a Ghost Town," *Desert Magazine*, 16 (July, 1953), 14-18.

_____, "Trail of the Master Muleskinners," *Westways*, 48 (October, 1956), 18-19.

Weight, Lucille, "Dorsey," *Desert Magazine*, 24 (May, 1961), 38-39.

"Where Calico Once Thrived," *Touring Topics*, 18 (May, 1925), 30-34.

Wright, Kate H., "The Cemetery at Calico," *The Pony*, 3 (April, 1936), 10.

Manuscripts

Loe, Bernard E., "An Analysis of the Economic Significance of Mojave Desert-Death Valley Borax Mining Operations, 1872-1963." Unpublished master's thesis,

University of Redlands, 1963.

Starr, Warren Dean, "History of the Settlement and Development of Calico, California, to 1900." Unpublished master's thesis, Washington State University, 1963.

Storms, W. H., "The Calico Gold Mine." Manuscript copy of an article of the same title appearing in *The American Mining Review*, November 21,1908. Lent to the author by J.T.Weakely of Los Angeles.

Timmons, Virgie, "Early Days in Daggett." Manuscript in possession of author, 1949.

Waitman, Leonard B., "The History of Camp Cady." Unpublished master's thesis, University of Redlands, 1953.

Weeks, F. B., "Possibilities of the Calico Mining District." Unpublished, undated manuscript of article of the same title published by the *Mining and Scientific Press*, May, 1925. Lent to the author by J. T. Weakely.

Woodman, Ruth C., "The History of the Pacific Coast Borax Company," Chapters VI, VII, VIII. Unpublished manuscript, 1969. In Ruth Woodman Papers, Department of Special Collections, Library, University of Oregon.

_____, Harold E. Noble, Homer McCoy, John K. Butler, Robert S. Samuels, Joe Tiffenbach, Dorrell McGowan, Elsa K. Jensen, "Death Valley Days" [scripts, series variously titled, 1930-1975]. Syndicated series, produced 1951-1975 in 558 episodes; released in fall 1952. North Hollywood: Filmaster Productions, 1959-1965. Unpublished manuscripts. Ruth Woodman Papers, Special Collections, Library, University of Oregon.

Maps

Baltazar, Alan F., "The Calico Cemetery." Appendix 4, *Calico and the Calico Mining District, 1881-1907*. Barstow: Alan Baltazar, 1995.

Dunlap, S. D., U. S. Deputy Surveyor, "MAP OF CALICO TOWN SITE," filed January 18,1883. San Bernardino County Archives.

McCulloch, T. H. "Geologic map of the Nebo and Yermo Quadrangles, San Bernardino County, California. Los Angeles Office, United States Geological Survey, open file map, 1965.

"Map of Calico." Unpublished, undated, typed listing of locations of structures along Calico Street. San Bernardino County Archives.

United States, Geological Survey. United States Coast and Geodetic Survey, 1953. Aerial Photos, 1951. Daggett Quadrangle 7.5 minute series, 15 minute series, San Bernardino County, California, Yermo Quadrangle, 7.5 minute series, San Bernardino County, California. Washington: Government Printing Office, 1953.

INDEX

About the Author

DOUGLAS STEEPLES is Professor of History and Dean at Mercer University. His primary research interest is the American West and U.S. business history after the Civil War. His most recent book is *Democracy in Desperation* (Greenwood, 1998).

ISBN 0-313-30836-5

90000>

EAN

9 780313 308369

HARDCOVER BAR CODE